# FROM THE
# KITCHENS OF SEVILLE

Visiting Spain through Authentic Recipes

Compiled by

Beth Matthews

Innovo
Publishing

Published by
Innovo Publishing LLC
www.innovopublishing.com
1-888-546-2111

Providing Full-Service Publishing Services for
Christian Authors, Artists & Organizations: Hardbacks, Paperbacks,
eBooks, Audiobooks, Music & Videos.

**FROM THE KITCHENS OF SEVILLE**

ISBN 13: 978-1-936076-49-9
ISBN 10: 1-936076-49-7

Cover Design & Interior Layout: Innovo Publishing LLC
Cover Photo: David Luque

Printed in the United States of America
U.S. Printing History

First Edition: December 2010

With appreciation to my two sons, Peter and Sam,

who did all of the original typing,

and to my husband Chris,

who encouraged and spearheaded this revision.

# Serving Up Food in Sevilla

This cookbook was compiled in a region of southern Spain called Andalucía. Ever since the first edition quickly sold out, we have been begged to issue another. At last, we have set aside work commitments to take up the pleasurable task of helping you learn about, or finally find, those genuine Spanish recipes you once tried on a trip to Spain, or that you had heard about for so long. This edition not only incorporated some other very homey recipes that we couldn't include in the first, but also enhanced some of the existing recipe instructions to make them more understandable. As before, ingredients were exactly the same or as close to the original as possible so as to help you experience results comparable to "the real thing."

As Andalucía's capital, Seville (or "Sevilla" in Spanish), is a classic European city with old time charm and incredibly satisfying food. Inside these pages you will find tried and true recipes that are, in many cases, centuries old. After various shorter trips to Spain over many years, our family moved to Sevilla twelve years ago and has enjoyed meal after meal with friends in their homes. At times our own guests return to the States with ingredients for a certain dish, trying to replicate the unique and exquisite flavors they found here.

After describing to Spanish friends and neighbors the type of book we wanted to make, one with everyday authentic recipes (but definitely not a coffee table cookbook), our Sevillano friends eagerly jumped into the task of telling us what kinds of food we should highlight. So, this cookbook comprises what many local Spaniards thought ought to be in it. Men and women alike opened drawers full of aging recipes (written in the script of grandmothers and great-aunts), found cookbooks cracking in the bindings, or just sat and recited from memory the ingredients for this sauté or that salad. Since we were striving for accuracy in measurements, and they were saying just to add a handful of rice or a dollop of sauce, we decided to measure out each handful and dollop. These same Spaniards now tell us they can't wait to hear how much you will enjoy using these recipes. They included some recipes such as Marinated Olives so that you can learn how the dish is prepared, even if you don't have olive trees in your yard like we do. If you were here, they would invite you in for a visit and cook your favorite dish for you!

Typically, Spanish kitchens are small and uncomplicated. Up until the recent past, ovens were a luxury; so even today, most cooks rely on a pressure cooker, a fryer, and a hand-held blender, and then sautéing, boiling, or frying on a gas stovetop to prepare all they need. Being a very Mediterranean diet, you stand to gain healthy ideas by using this, their book of recipes. So decide on a menu, and get started!

Note that this is a "working" cookbook, meaning we left extra-wide margins for you to scribble your own variations, thoughts, or time and place you tried a certain recipe. We trust that over the years this book will become a well-loved favorite.

# Andalucía: Land of Many Cultures, Sunshine, and Olive Trees

Andalucía originally was settled by the Tartessians, an ancient race who had early contact with the Phoenicians. That the area's value was widely known was seen in the fact that King Solomon of the Old Testament sent over trading ships to bring back silver, peacocks, ivory and apes. A Greek mariner named Hercules founded the capital city of Sevilla over two thousand years ago. Later, the Romans brought olive trees, and built their ubiquitous roads, bridges and aqueducts. The Romans were driven out by Gothic tribes from Northern Germany who left behind cathedrals and monuments. In the eighth century, the North African Arab tribes invaded, conquering the southern half of the peninsula.

The Arabs perfected the use of mathematics, science, architecture and agriculture in this region for eight hundred years until ousted by northern Spaniards in 1492. Since then, many Andalucíans (beginning with Christopher Columbus' help) looked to the New World, trying to win their fortune in the Americas. Andalucía currently is an autonomous region in the kingdom of Spain.

All this mixing of cultures has caused a curious blending of the best of many lands. Andalucíans are historically known for beautiful horses, lively dancing, zesty guitar music, siestas and fiestas, lovely women, brave men and traditional religious festivals. They start their day around 8 a.m. with a quick cup of coffee and head to work. Mid-morning, they will get toast (made from the small or larger loaves of dense Spanish baguettes, each variety with its own name) and more coffee then head back to work until 2 p.m. Everyone leaves work, school and duties to eat a large lunch at home from 2 to 5 p.m. (the siesta, don't forget). Back to work from 5 to 8 p.m., with time out for a dish of tapas (always with different varieties of olives at hand) to hold them over until a lighter supper meal around 10 p.m. in the winter, and even later in the summer. That amounts to eating five times per day, so no wonder Andalucíans have plenty of food dishes to share!

Several times per year they celebrate holy days and hold town fairs, called ferias. Some of the recipes you will find here come from these events. One of the appealing things about Andalucían life is that families tend to eat together at least twice per day. Most Andalucíans also like to go out to the country for picnics and down to the beach for the day to soak up the generous sunshine. They will pack lighter meals like some of those you will find in this book that travel well and do not need refrigeration. Even in those meals, you will always find a variety of olives for snacking.

Andalucía is a delightful place to live with warm and generous people. We hope you will find in the recipes a reflection of their sunshine.

# Table of Contents

# APPETIZERS
# &
# BEVERAGES

# Salmon and Cheese Canapés

*(Salmón Marinado con Queso)*

| | |
|---|---|
| 2 lbs. coarse salt | ½ spring onion, chopped |
| 1 lb. sugar | 2 lbs. raw salmon, filleted |
| ⅛ tsp. ginger | 1 lb. soft fresh cheese slices |
| ½ tsp. dill | |

Mix all ingredients but salmon in a bowl. Spread out half of the ingredients in a large glass baking dish. Place salmon fillets on top, being careful not place on top of each other. Pour rest of marinade ingredients on top of the fillets. Cover and refrigerate 1-2 days. Salmon is now "cured" and must be cleaned. Rinse under running water and pat dry with paper towels. Cut in smaller pieces. Lay a salmon piece on top of a cheese slice to eat. Do not cook. Serves 8-10.

*Carmen del Bot*

# Marinated Olives

*(Aceitunas Aliñadas)*

*Preserving Olives*

| | |
|---|---|
| 5 gal. green olives fresh off the tree | 5 qt. water |
| 1 c. lye crystals | 2 lbs. salt |

Pick olives off tree once they are soft and ripe. Separate the green, less mature ones, from the riper black ones. In a clean plastic bucket large enough to hold all the greener olives, dissolve lye crystals in water, using 8 oz. per 5 quarts water. Mix well with a plastic or wooden stirrer. Water will heat. Let cool. Carefully pour olives into lye water and cover with a sheet of plastic and weight the plastic with a dish so as to assure that all olives are soaking and not floating above the water. Let stand 6-7 hours. After olives have soaked, remove one olive and slice into it (being careful not to touch the lye to anything it could stain), and see if the olive is tender throughout. If so, remove olives into another clean bucket and begin to rinse thoroughly. Drain discarded lye water into a sink, being careful not to splash. After olives have been well-rinsed, make a salt water solution in another bucket. Put in enough water to cover olives (but don't actually put olives in yet). Put a raw egg in the water.

# Marinated Olives

## (Aceitunas Aliñadas)

Begin stirring in salt, dissolving it well. When the egg begins to float, the water is salty enough. Remove egg. Put in olives. Lay a film of plastic over the water and gently weight it down to hold olives in the solution. Let sit for 40 days. Rinse and set aside olives while draining and cleaning the bucket. Make a new salt water solution as before. Place olives back in. The olives can now be eaten, or they can be marinated.

*Marinating Olives*

| | |
|---|---|
| 5 bay leaves | 2 lemon quarters |
| 5 carrot slices | 2 tsp. oregano |
| 1 tsp. thyme | 2 T. sliced green pepper |
| 4 cloves garlic, whole | |

For every quart of olives and salt water, stir in the ingredients listed above. Seal in bottles or refrigerate.

*Dora Ruíz Ortíz*

# Christmas Eve Shrimp

## (Gambas de Nochebuena)

| | |
|---|---|
| 2 lbs. shrimp, whole in shell | salted water |
| 2 bay leaves | 2 T. coarse salt |

Bring water and bay leaves to a boil. Place shrimp in boiling water for 1-2 minutes. Drain and rinse with fresh cool water. Arrange shrimp parallel on a lettuce covered platter and sprinkle salt over all. Serves 4-6.

*Paula Pérez Benítez*

# Shrimp

## (Gambas)

| | |
|---|---|
| 1 c. olive oil | 2 lbs. cleaned shrimp |
| 3 heads garlic, cleaned and minced | 1 T. coarse salt |
| 1 small hot chili pepper | *(continued)* |

# Shrimp

*(Gambas)*

*(continued)* Sauté garlic until soft. Add the whole chili pepper to the sauté. Add shrimp, spreading out all. Salt to taste. Leave a minute in pan, then arrange all on a platter and serve. Serves 4-6.

*Carmen del Bot*

# Clams in Tomato Sauce

*(Almejas al Tomate)*

½ c. olive oil
1 lb. clams in the shell
1 med. onion
¾ c. bits of cured ham

½ c. white wine
½ c. tomato sauce
salt to taste

In frying pan, heat oil and sauté onions. Drop in washed clams. Heat over medium heat. Shells will open during the cooking process. Add in ham and wine and stir. Heat for 2-3 minutes, then add tomato sauce. Simmer for 5 minutes. Serves 4-6.

*Joaquina Berengena García*

# Spanish Escargot

*(Cabrillas)*

1 lb. large snails
¼ lb. tomatoes
½ green bell pepper
¼ onion, chopped
6 cloves garlic, minced
1 bay leaf
1 T. fresh parsley, snipped
pinch red pepper
½ tsp. cumin

½ tsp. cilantro
½ tsp. black pepper
¼ tsp. cloves
¼ c. olive oil
½ c. cooking wine
salt to taste
½ baguette, cut in pieces and
 fried in oil

# Spanish Escargot

## (Cabrillas)

Wash snails well and let rest 1 hour. Put snails in pot, cover with water and bring to boil. When water begins to boil, take off heat and rinse snails again. In a separate frying pan, sauté all the vegetables and spices in the oil and wine until golden. Purée in blender. Return to frying pan and add snails. Stir, cooking for 5 minutes. If snails are not completely submerged in liquid, add water just to cover. Bring to boil, letting simmer covered for 20 minutes. Finally, add the fried bread pieces and let cook 10 minutes more. Serves 6-8.

*Asunción Romero Gazo*

# Marinated Carrots

## (Zanahorias Cocidas Frías)

| | |
|---|---|
| 1 lb. carrots, peeled and cooked | 1 tsp. salt |
| 3 cloves garlic, minced | 1 T. vinegar |
| ½ tsp. cumin | 1½ tsp. olive oil |
| 1 T. parsley | |

Cut carrots into 1-inch chunks. In separate smaller bowl, mix marinade ingredients all together. Pour over carrots, then stir and chill. Serves 10.

*Joaquina Berengena García*

# Marinated Beets

## (Remolacha)

| | |
|---|---|
| 1 lb. cooked beets, sliced | 1 T. olive oil |
| ½ onion, chopped | 1 tsp. salt |
| 1 T. vinegar | |

Put beets in a bowl. Mix marinade ingredients. Pour over beets and let sit in refrigerator until well-chilled. Serves 10.

*Joaquina Berengena García*

# Bread and Cheese

*(Pan con Queso)*

8 oz. hard, cured goat or sheep
    cheese (Manchego)

2 c. olive oil
1 baguette of bread

Cut cheese into small cubes. Marinate cheese in a bowl with oil for 24 hours. Later cut bread into small, thick slices and place one cheese cube on each slice. Serves 4.

*Rosa Garrido Serrano*

# Filled Eggs

*(Huevos Rellenos)*

4 hard-boiled eggs
4 oz. canned tuna
½ tsp. salt

3 T. of recipe for Ali-Oli Mayonnaise
2 lettuce leaves, chopped fine

Split eggs in half length-wise and remove yolks. Set egg whites aside on a platter. Put yolks in a bowl and add tuna, lettuce, Ali-Oli mayonnaise and salt. Blend until creamy. Fill egg whites with this mixture and chill. Serves 4.

*Rosa Garrido Serrano*

# Snow Men

*(Hombres de Nieve)*

1 recipe for filled eggs
4 toothpicks

4 green olives
4 long red pimento strips

Slice ¼ inch off the larger, more rounded end of each egg. This is the snowman's cap. Set aside. Make recipes for Filled Eggs. After filling, place the two halves back together and set upright on the end that is now flat. Insert a toothpick into one of the ends of an olive, through the hole where the pit was removed. Let protrude only a very little bit on one end. Insert the long end of the toothpick in between the 2 egg halves, taking care not to force it back open. Leave the green olive (which will represent the head) on the top of the egg.

# Snow Men

---

*(Hombres de Nieve)*

Make the cap by taking the small white egg slice and anchoring the flat side to the toothpick protruding from the top of the olive. Wrap the long pimento strip (or scarf), around the snowman's neck (between the olive and the egg). Snowman should now have a stuffed egg sitting on end as his body, an olive for a head attached by a toothpick going through the body; a white egg slice cap attached to the tiny toothpick poking out the other end of the olive; and a red pimento scarf wrapped around his neck. Repeat procedure for other eggs. Serves 4.

*Rosa Garrido Serrano*

# Coffee with Milk

---

*(Café con Leche)*

1 c. water
3-4 T. ground coffee

1 c. whole milk
1-3 tsp. sugar

Heat milk to scalding, but do not boil. Make coffee in espresso coffeemaker with above amounts of coffee and water. Pour coffee into two cups, divide milk between the two cups, and add 1-3 tsp. of sugar per cup. Stir well. Serves 2.

*Paula Pérez Benítez*

# Hot Chocolate for Churros

---

*(Chocolate para Churros)*

1 c. whole milk
2 tsp. cocoa
1 ½ T. sugar

1 oz. milk chocolate
1 T. cornstarch
dash salt

Dissolve cornstarch in milk. Heat milk in saucepan, stirring in cocoa. Stir over medium-low heat until thickened. Add in milk chocolate, sugar and salt, stirring until dissolved. Serves 1.

*Tere Bernal*

# Sangría Summer Fruit Drink

## (Sangría)

2 c. either sweet red wine or
    red grape juice
8 c. orange soda
1 whole lemon, chopped
1 whole orange, chopped
3 peaches, pitted, peeled and
    chopped

¼ honeydew melon fruit,
    peeled and chopped
1 apple, peeled and chopped
1 stick cinnamon
6 cloves
2 T. sugar (if using red wine)
2 T. gin

Mix in a large pitcher 2 hours before serving. Serves 10-16.

*María Carmen Luque Martínez*


# Strawberry Milkshake

## (Batido de Fresa)

1-2 pt. ripe strawberries
1 qt. whole milk

¼ c. sugar

Wash and chop strawberries well. Purée in blender. Add milk and sugar and blend again. Serves 4.

*Salud Borrego Méndez*

# SOUPS

# &

# SALADS

# Gómez Family Gazpacho

*(Gazpacho)*

3 cloves garlic
2-3 green bell peppers, seeded
½ cucumber, peeled
5 ripe tomatoes, peeled
1 loaf hard baguette
1 T. red wine vinegar

¼ c. olive oil
2 tsp. salt
garnishes: cucumber,
    onion, hard-boiled egg,
    cured ham bits,
    croutons (all chopped)

    Blend first 3 ingredients with 2 tomatoes and set aside in large bowl. Blend remaining ingredients, combine and stir. Strain to remove any chunks or peels. Chill very cold. Top with any of the above garnishes as desired. Serves 6.

*Jonatán Gómez Martínez.*

# Andalucían Gazpacho

*(Gazpacho Andaluz)*

1 green bell pepper
1 cucumber
3 lbs. red ripe tomatoes
2 cloves garlic
1 tsp. coarse salt
⅓ c. red wine vinegar
1 c. olive oil

1 fist-sized piece of baguette,
    moistened
1 apple, quartered or carrot,
    peeled (optional)
garnishes: bits of egg, ham,
    minced parsley and drizzled
    olive oil

    Put all in blender and purée. Strain out any peel and seeds. Chill very cold, top with garnishes of choice. Serves 6-8.

*Lola Mesa Rodríguez*

# White Gazpacho

*(Gazpacho de Ajo Blanco)*

¼ c. blanched almonds
3 cloves garlic
1 c. fresh bread crumbs
¼ c. olive oil

1½ tsp. vinegar
3 glasses water, salted with 3 tsp. salt
garnish: white grapes

# White Gazpacho

*(Gazpacho de Ajo Blanco)*

Pulverize almonds in mortar or sturdy bowl. Set aside. Mash garlic well and add to almonds. Crumble the bread, but don't use the crust. Add bread to almonds and garlic. Stir in olive oil to mixture until a liquid paste is formed. Add vinegar, blend well. Stir in the cold salted water until smooth. Once served in bowls, garnish with white grapes. Serves 4-6.

*Joaquina Berengena García*

# Eduardo's Summer Soup

*(Salmorejo)*

3 lbs. red-ripe tomatoes
2 cloves garlic
1 tsp. coarse salt
1 c. olive oil
1 fist-sized chunk of day-old baguette
½ c. icy cold water
⅓ red wine vinegar

Purée all but water in a blender and then pass through a strainer to get out any leftover seeds or pulp. Add cold water and blend well. Serves 6.

*Eduardo Pérez González*

# Creamy Summer Soup

*(Salmorejo)*

2 lbs. tomatoes, peeled, quartered
1 clove garlic
1 red pepper, seeded, quartered
1 apple, cored, quartered
1 fist-sized chunk of day-old baguette
2 T. olive oil
1 T. red wine vinegar (or)
1 T. lemon juice
garnishes: bacon bits, hard-boiled eggs

Purée all in a blender. Chill well. Garnish with bits of bacon or hard-boiled egg. Serves 4-6.

*Joaquina Berengena García*

# Lentil Stew

*(Potaje de Lentejas)*

1 c. dried lentils
1 link chorizo sausage, halved
2 T. olive oil
3-4 cloves garlic, whole and peeled
2 small, whole potatoes, peeled
1 medium onion, halved
1 small, whole tomato

1 green bell pepper, halved
1 bay leaf
½ tsp. paprika
1-2 carrots, sliced
2 cubes chicken bouillon
2 tsp. salt
pinch black pepper

Soak lentils in cold water to cover in a large pot for 30 minutes before cooking. Drain off water. Cook sausage separately in a little pan 5-10 minutes to remove excess fat. Add drained sausage to lentils. Add all ingredients to pot, except for bouillon, salt and pepper. Cover with water to 1 inch above level of ingredients, and bring to boil. Let simmer 20 minutes. Add bouillon, salt and pepper. Cut potatoes in chunks once softened. Stirring occasionally, cook 20 minutes more and serve. Serves 4-6.

*Luisa Márquez Vázquez*

# Consommé

*(Puchero)*

¼ c. dried chickpeas
1 Anaheim green pepper
1 potato
1 sm. onion
1 carrot
3-oz. piece of salt pork

1 chicken leg quarter
½ lb. beef or pork stew meat
2 oz. salted aged beef or pork rib
4 oz. salted aged pork back bone
1 soup beef bone
3-oz. piece of cured beef or pork

Soak chickpeas overnight. Drain the next day. Along with chickpeas, put all ingredients in a stock pot. Add water to just below level of contents. Bring to boil and then simmer one hour. Afterwards, strain out all solids from the consommé, setting them aside for other use, or discard. Pour stock into containers and freeze. Thaw for use as consommé when desired. Makes 2-3 quarts.

*Luisa Márquez Vázquez*

# Seafood Soup

*(Sopa de Marisco)*

water
2 lbs. filleted white hake or
    haddock
1 lb. filleted monkfish
½ lb. raw shrimp, peeled
½ lb. clams
½ c. olive oil
2 ripe tomatoes, chopped

2 cloves garlic, minced
1 green bell pepper, chopped
½ onion, chopped
1 sprig fresh parsley, chopped
4 oz. angel hair pasta, broken
    fine
salt to taste

    In a large stock pot, put 2½ quarts of salted water. Cook over medium heat all seafood (except for shrimp) for 20 minutes. Add shrimp during the last minute. Strain all seafood from the water; reserve stock and set aside. Clean seafood under running water, and return to stock. Add pasta to stock. Bring to boil and let cook 5 minutes. In frying pan, heat oil. Sauté all vegetables and parsley, stirring throughout for 15 minutes. Strain vegetables out of oil and pass through a food mill or strainer. Add to the stock with the seafood. Once hot throughout, salt and serve. Serves 6.

*María Carmen Luque Martínez*


# Cream of Zucchini Soup

*(Puré de Calabacín)*

2 large zucchini (may substitute
    1 lb. peeled fresh pumpkin)
1 med. potato, peeled
3 pkts. triangular foil wrapped
    soft white cheese, such as
    Laughing Cow® cheese

garnishes: hard-boiled egg slices,
    croutons, cured ham bits
1 onion (if using zucchini)
salt to taste

    Boil zucchini (or pumpkin), potato, and onion in salted water until soft. Remove from water and purée in blender, adding 3 cheese triangles. Reheat if necessary. Top with preferred garnishes. Serves 2-4.

*Dora Ruíz Ortíz*

# Vichyssoise Cream Soup

*(Crema Vichyssoise)*

2 leeks, cut up
2 zucchini, cut up
2 med. potatoes, cut up
½ c. light cream

4 triangles of foil wrapped soft
   cheese
pinch black pepper
1 T. butter

Cook the vegetables in salted water until soft. Drain water. Purée vegetables in blender, adding cream, cheese, pepper and butter. Serve hot. Serves 4.

*Joaquina Berengena García*

# Adela's Veggie Soup

*(Crema de Verduras)*

2 potatoes, peeled
1 onion
4 carrots
2 c. chicken broth

2 c. water
1 c. light cream
pinch black pepper
1 branch parsley, snipped

Chop vegetables. Cook in saucepan in chicken broth and water until tender. Remove from heat and let cool 10 minutes. Strain vegetables from pot. Purée vegetables in a blender, adding back in liquid from stock necessary to make it creamy. Add cream and pepper. Mix well. Once in bowls, sprinkle with parsley. Serves 4.

*Adela Pineda Camino*

# Hot Tomato Soup

*(Sopa de Tomate)*

24 oz. hard round bread
1-1½ lbs. tomatoes, diced
1 green bell pepper, diced fine
2 cloves garlic, minced

⅓ c. olive oil
water
salt
1 sprig of fresh mint

# Hot Tomato Soup

*(Sopa de Tomate)*

Thinly slice bread and set aside. Heat oil in a frying pan. Add vegetables and lightly brown. Add bread slices, stirring to mix well. Add enough water to just below level of vegetables. Stir in salt. Add mint and stir gently. Serves 4-6.

*Joaquina Berengena García*

# Classic Salad

*(Ensalada)*

1 head Romaine lettuce
½ onion, julienne slices
2 firm tomatoes, not quite ripe, sliced

½ c. olive oil
2 T. red wine vinegar
coarse salt

Clean lettuce, trimming unsightly parts. Place on platter, topped with onion and tomato. Drizzle oil and vinegar over. Sprinkle on salt. Serves 6-8.

*María José Guerrero Abril*

# Mixed Salad

*(Ensalada Mixta)*

1 recipe Classic Salad
2 hard-boiled eggs, sliced
½ cucumber, chopped
1 carrot, grated

6 white asparagus spears
3 T. cold canned corn
¼ c. tuna fish
12 green olives

Decorate the Classic Salad with any or all of the above garnishes. Add more olive oil, vinegar and salt to taste. Serves 6-8.

*María José Guerrero Abril*

# Watercress and Beet Salad

## (Ensalada de Remolacha)

3 bunches watercress
2 beets
4 tomatoes, peeled

2 hard-boiled eggs, peeled
1 recipe All-Purpose Vinaigrette
salt

Rinse and dry the watercress and beets well. Place beets in boiling water and let cook until tender. Remove beets from hot water and let cool. Peel and dice them. Slice the tomatoes and eggs. Arrange watercress on a platter. Set eggs and beets on top of greens. Drizzle with the All-Purpose Vinaigrette dressing. Arrange tomatoes around edges of platter. Serves 4-6.

*Chelo Gómez Sánchez*

# Diced Salad

## (Picadillo)

1 onion, chopped
2 tomatoes, chopped
2 Anaheim green peppers, chopped

1 tsp. salt
¼ c. olive oil
2 T. vinegar

Put all vegetables in a salad bowl and mix. Stir together salt, oil and vinegar and drizzle over salad. Serves 4-6.

*María Carmen Luque Martínez*

# Marinated Salad

## (Aliño)

1 recipe Diced Salad
4 hard-boiled eggs, sliced
2 potatoes, boiled and diced
2 small cans tuna in oil

½ c. olives, green or black
½ c. codfish eggs, cooked and
  sliced

To the Diced Salad, choose and add any or all of the above ingredients desired, increasing the salt, oil and vinegar amounts proportionately. Serves 6-8.

*María Carmen Luque Martínez*

# Tomato Slices

*(Lonchas de Tomate)*

coarse salt
2 large firm tomatoes
⅓ c. olive oil

1 T. oregano
½ c. grated mozzarella cheese

Slice tomatoes ¼ inch thick, and lay out on a platter. Sprinkle salt over. Drizzle oil over. Sprinkle oregano over and let sit 5 minutes. Sprinkle cheese over and serve. Serves 3-4.

*Paula Pérez Benítez*

# Marinated Roe Salad

*(Aliño de Huevas)*

1 lb. roe from cod or hake
1 lb. red ripe, tomatoes, chopped
2 green bell peppers, chopped
1-2 large spring onions, chopped

1 cucumber, chopped
1 T. vinegar
¼ c. olive oil
coarse salt

Put the oblong-shaped roe in salted water and boil for 30-35 minutes. Remove from water. Slice into ½ inch rounds, and arrange on a platter. Set aside. In a bowl, mix the chopped vegetables. Dress with the vinegar, oil and salt. Arrange vegetables by the spoonful on top of the roe, pouring the rest of the dressing over. Chill and serve. Serves 6-8.

*Paula Pérez Benítez*

# Corn and Sausage Salad

*(Ensalada de Salchicha y Maíz)*

4 frankfurters, cut up
4 oz. cooked corn
1 onion, chopped
2-3 gherkins, chopped

2 oz. red pimentos, chopped
2 T. olive oil
1 T. vinegar
1 T. mustard

Mix meat and vegetables. Stir in dressing and chill until ready to serve. Serves 4.

Adela Pineda Camino

# Seafood Splash

---

*(Salpicón)*

1 onion, chopped
2 tomatoes, diced
2 Anaheim green peppers, chopped
½ lb. cooked crab leg meat
½ lb. cooked shrimp, cleaned

1 lb. cooked mild white fish, in chunks
coarse salt
½ c. olive oil
3 T. red wine vinegar

Mix vegetables together first, set aside. Lay seafood in the bottom of a 9" x 13" pan. Place vegetables over top of seafood. Mix oil, salt, and vinegar together in a cup and pour over all. Let chill in refrigerator 2-3 hours before serving. Serves 4-6.

*María Carmen Luque Martínez*


# Russian Salad

---

*(Ensaladilla Rusa)*

salted water
2 lbs. potatoes, peeled and diced
3 carrots, peeled and diced
¾ c. peas
1 tsp. salt

1 T. vinegar
1½ c. mayonnaise, separated
garnishes: pimentos, sliced hard-boiled eggs, peas and olives

Boil potatoes and carrots together 15 minutes, adding peas the last 2-3 minutes. Drain water. Cool vegetables. Add salt and vinegar. Stir in 1 cup mayonnaise. Turn vegetables out onto a platter, and form into a rounded or square shape 2 inches high. Spread top and sides with remaining ½ cup mayonnaise. Decorate with any of above garnishes. Chill well. Serves 4-6.

*María Carmen Luque Martínez*

# Marinated Chickpeas

*(Aliño de Garbanzos)*

1 lb. chickpeas, soaked overnight in salt water
4-5 tomatoes, peeled and diced
2 Anaheim green peppers, finely chopped
1 onion, minced
6-8 oz. tuna in olive oil
4 hard-boiled eggs, chopped
1 tsp. salt
¼ c. olive oil
¼ c. red wine vinegar

Cook chickpeas until tender. Drain and then chill in a large bowl. Add tomatoes, peppers and onions. Stir in tuna and mix well. Add eggs to bowl and gently stir. Mix the salt, oil and vinegar in a bowl, then drizzle over chickpeas. Serves 8-10.

*Tere Bernal*

# Rice and Tuna Salad

*(Ensalada de Arroz)*

1 c. rice
2 c. water
2 T. olive oil, for sautéing
1 clove garlic, minced
10 black olives, halved
3-4 oz. canned tuna, drained
1 sm. onion, chopped
2 sm. tomatoes, diced
1 T. vinegar
2 T. olive oil, for dressing
1 T. coarse salt

Bring water to boil in saucepan, add rice and cook on low for 20 minutes. Then let cool. Sauté garlic in 2 T. oil. Put rice in a bowl and add garlic and all other ingredients, mixing well. Chill. Serves 4-6.

*Joaquina Berengena García*

# VEGETABLES

# &

# SIDE DISHES

# Country-Style Potatoes

*(Patatas a lo Pobre)*

2 lbs. potatoes, peeled, sliced
   in ¼ inch rounds
1½ tsp. salt
⅓ c. olive oil
2 cloves garlic, minced

1 stalk fresh parsley, minced
1½ tsp. red wine vinegar
3 T. water
1 egg

     Put sliced potato rounds in a bowl and salt well. Heat oil in a frying pan. Put in potatoes and cook until soft over medium-low heat in covered pan. When potatoes become soft, add garlic, parsley, and vinegar. Add water and let simmer 5 minutes. Crack one egg over the pan and let fall into potatoes so as to break the yolk. Stir egg around slightly and serve. Serves 4-6.

*Joaquina Berengena García*

# Feisty Potatoes

*(Patatas Bravas)*

2 lbs. potatoes, peeled, diced
1½ qt. water
salt

2 c. mayonnaise
3 cloves garlic, mashed
parsley

     Cut potatoes in large squares and cook in boiling salted water. When soft, drain water and put potatoes in large bowl. Crush garlic and mix with mayonnaise. Mix into potatoes. Spread on a platter and sprinkle with parsley. Serves 4-6.

*Paula Pérez Benítez*

# Consommé Chickpeas with Spinach

*(Espinacas con Garbanzos de Puchero)*

16 oz. frozen chopped spinach
½ c. olive oil
3-5 cloves of garlic
½ c. chickpeas, previously
cooked in Consommé

¼ tsp. paprika
⅛ tsp. each of cilantro,
   paprika, cayenne pepper,
   cumin, salt
salt to taste

# Consommé Chickpeas with Spinach

*(Espinacas con Garbanzos de Puchero)*

Reserve chickpeas out of the Recipe for Consommé. Cook spinach in salted water according to package directions. Drain. In hot olive oil, lightly brown garlic slices. Stir in paprika and other spices. Add spinach, stirring as well. Add in drained chickpeas and stir well. Serves 2-3.

*Luisa Márquez Vásquez*

# Sautéed Vegetables

*(Pipirana)*

| | |
|---|---|
| ½ c. olive oil | 1 lb. zucchini, peeled and |
| 1 clove garlic | chopped |
| 1 lb. eggplant, peeled and | 2 lbs. tomatoes, chopped |
| chopped | salt to taste |

Sauté whole garlic clove in hot oil in frying pan, until soft. Remove and set aside. Sauté eggplant and zucchini until soft. Remove and set aside. Add more oil if necessary. Sauté tomatoes 2 minutes. Put all vegetables back in pan, salt, mix well, serve. Serves 4-6.

*Joaquina Berengena García*

# Vegetable Sauté

*(Pisto)*

| | |
|---|---|
| 2 zucchinis | 1 onion |
| 2 eggplants, peeled | 2 cloves garlic |
| ½ lb. fresh pumpkin, peeled | 15-oz. can crushed tomatoes |
| ½ lb. fresh green bean, ends | olive oil for sautéing |
| snapped off | |

Chop all fresh vegetables. Sauté each separately in a heavy pan in a little olive oil until soft, setting aside each while the next sautés. Return all to pan with crushed tomatoes, adding enough water to keep vegetables from being dry. Salt as needed. Serves 4-6.

*Encarni Domínguez Ledesma*

# Zucchini Eggplant Sauté

*(Berenjena con Calabacín)*

½ c. olive oil
1 oz. onion, chopped
1 zucchini, peeled and diced
1 eggplant, peeled and diced
1 tsp. flour

½ tsp. black pepper
2 chicken bouillon cubes
2 c. water
¼ c. white wine (optional)

Sauté the onion in hot oil until golden. Add in zucchini and eggplant, sautéing 5 minutes. Sprinkle in flour and pepper, stir well. Add bouillon and water, cook until all tender and water reduced. Add wine the last 5 minutes if desired. Serves 4-6.

*Joaquina Berengena García*

# White Beans

*(Habichuelas)*

1 lb. white navy or kidney beans,
    soaked
1 red pepper, seeded
1 tomato
3 cloves garlic
1 bay leaf

½ tsp. red pepper (or)
½ tsp. paprika
4 oz. chorizo sausage
2 T. olive oil
salt to taste

Soak beans overnight in water. Next day, drain, and put beans in a large pot with fresh cold water, bringing up to the level of the beans. Add in all other ingredients and let simmer for 20-30 minutes or until beans are soft. Serves 4-6.

*Joaquina Berengena García*

# Breaded Eggplant
# with Ham and Cheese

*(Berenjena Empanada)*

1 large or 2 small eggplant(s)
mild white cheese slices
boiled or cured ham slices
1-2 c. bread crumbs

2-3 eggs, beaten
salt
oil for frying

# Breaded Eggplant
# with Ham and Cheese

*(Berenjena Empanada)*

Slice eggplant in ¼ inch slices. Heat oil for frying in frying pan. Between two slices of eggplant, place one slice each of ham and cheese. Moisten "sandwich" with egg then dip in bread crumbs to thoroughly coat. Fry several at a time, letting brown on both sides. Drain on paper towel and salt to taste. Serves 4-6.

*María Carmen Luque Martínez*

# Fried Eggplant with Molasses

*(Berenjena con Miel de Caña)*

| | |
|---|---|
| 2 eggplants, sliced thin | 1 tsp. salt |
| 2 c. vegetable oil | 2 eggs, beaten |
| 2 c. bread crumbs | ½ c. molasses |

Heat oil in frying pan. Coat eggplant slices one at a time, first in the bread crumbs in which salt has been mixed, once in the egg, then again in the bread crumbs, completely covering each slice. Fry in hot oil until golden brown on both sides. Drain on paper towel and set aside on platter. Once all eggplant slices have been breaded and fried and placed on platter, drizzle warmed molasses over all. Serves 4-6.

*Encarni Domínguez Ledesma*

# Stuffed Eggplant

*(Berenjena Rellena de Brandada)*

| | |
|---|---|
| ¾ lb. fresh cod | 1 tsp. salt |
| 1 c. milk | 1 clove garlic |
| 2 c. water | 4 oz. light cream |
| 2 eggplants | ⅛ tsp. black pepper |
| 1½ c. olive oil, divided | garnish: Tomato Sauce Recipe |

*(continued)*

# Stuffed Eggplant

---

*(Berenjena Rellena de Brandada)*

*(continued)* Cook cod in boiling milk and water for 5 minutes. Set aside. Cut eggplants in half and make cuts into them. Sprinkle ¼ c. olive oil and salt on these halves. Bake 15-20 minutes at 350°. Drain and clean cod, cutting in pieces into a bowl. Mash garlic and put in same bowl. Into the garlic/cod mixture, add 1 c. olive oil and cream, mixing all until paste is formed. Sprinkle pepper into bowl. Remove eggplant from oven and scrape out meat and mash. Reserve shells. In remaining ¼ c. oil, sauté eggplant in frying pan. Fill the eggplant shells with this mixture, then cover with the cod mixture. Brown in oven. Top with the recipe of heated Tomato Sauce. Serves 4-6.

*Joaquina Berengena García*

# Eggs in a Nest

---

*(Guisantes con Huevo)*

| | |
|---|---|
| ½ c. olive oil | 1 lb. frozen peas |
| 2 carrots, sliced | pinch saffron |
| 1 onion, chopped | ½ c. water |
| 2-3 cloves garlic, chopped | 4-6 eggs |
| 1 fresh tomato, peeled, crushed | |

In a large frying pan, sauté altogether the carrots, onion and garlic in hot oil. Let cook until tender, then add tomatoes; stir. Add peas with water. Sprinkle in saffron and stir. When peas are tender, open up 4-6 little holes, "nests", in among them, and crack one egg into each. Let cook, not stirring, until eggs are done. Serves 4-6.

*Salud Borrego Méndez*

# Little Garden Birds

---

*(Pajaritos de Huerta)*

| | |
|---|---|
| Anaheim green peppers, one per person | coarse salt |
| olive oil | |

# Little Garden Birds

## (Pajaritos de Huerta)

Clean and seed peppers, and dry off water. In the side of each pepper, push open a little hole with thumb. Put in this hole ½ tsp. of coarse salt. Pour 1 inch of oil in a frying pan and heat to medium-high. Fry peppers with the hole side up, until tender but not burnt. Drain well. Makes 1.

*María Carmen Luque Martínez*

# Roasted Sweet Peppers

## (Pimientos Asados)

| | |
|---|---|
| 2 red peppers | ¼ cup olive oil |
| 2 green peppers | Red wine vinegar |
| 2 Anaheim green peppers | Salt |

First method: Wash and core the peppers, but leave the rest whole. Place hot olive oil in a large frying pan over medium heat. Let brown slowly. Turn as necessary, but carefully, as oil may splatter. Remove when soft. Let cool, and carefully peel off skin. Place in a bowl and drizzle a little red wine vinegar over along with salt. May be eaten as is, all together as a salad, or used as a garnish.

Second method: Prepare peppers as above. Place in a casserole dish, and bake at 375 for up to one hour, depending on size of peppers. After soft and browned, remove from oven, let cool, and peel. Drizzle olive oil and vinegar over, and salt to taste.

*From several friends*

# Peppers San Jacobo

## (San Jacobo Pimientos)

| | |
|---|---|
| 1 lb. Anaheim green peppers | bread crumbs |
| 4 oz. sliced cheese | salt |
| 4 oz. Danish ham slices | oil for frying |
| 1-2 eggs | |

*(continued)*

# Peppers San Jacobo

*(San Jacobo Pimientos)*

*(continued)* Bake whole peppers on a baking sheet at 400°. When they soften (about 15-20 minutes), take out of oven, let cool. Cut off stem and halve each. In each half, place a slice of cheese and another of ham. Dip first in egg and then dredge in bread crumbs. Fry in hot oil until golden brown on each side. Drain on towels and then salt to taste. Serves 4-6.

*Carmen del Bot*

# Vegetables Esparragadas

*(Verduras Esparragadas)*

olive oil for sautéing
2-3 cloves garlic, sliced
⅓ c. fresh bread crumbs (don't use crust)
1 lb. frozen vegetable of choice

2 chicken bouillon cubes
water for moistening
1 tsp. paprika

Choose 1 lb. of a frozen vegetable (either spinach, artichoke hearts, lima beans, brussels sprouts or cabbage) and have them ready for later. Sauté garlic slices in hot oil until soft. Remove from oil and mash in a mortar or in a bowl with a fork until completely soft. Fry bread crumbs in same oil until crispy. Remove and also pulverize in mortar together with the bouillon cubes. Add enough water to be able to mix garlic, bread crumbs and bouillon into a mash. In same hot pan, add paprika to oil. Then place in vegetables and stir well. Spoon in bread crumb mixture and stir into vegetable. When the vegetable is tender, the dish is ready. Serves 4-6.

*Salud Borrego Méndez*

# Scrambled Beans

*(Revuelto de Judías)*

1 lb. green beans, cooked
1 large onion, minced
⅓ c. olive oil

salt
2 eggs
¼ tsp. vinegar

# Scrambled Beans

*(Revuelto de Judías)*

Boil beans if they are fresh. Sauté onions in olive oil in a frying pan. Drain green beans and add to sauté. Add in eggs, mix around well. Sprinkle vinegar over all. Serve hot. Serves 4-6.

*Joaquina Berengena García*

# Croquettes

*(Croquetas)*

4 T. olive oil
1 onion, chopped
¼ c. flour
2 c. milk
1 tsp. salt
2-3 mint leaves

pinch nutmeg
¾ c. either shredded cured
ham, chicken, beef (or)
minced shrimp, fish or crab
(or) cooked chopped
spinach

Sauté the onion in non-stick frying pan until soft. Sprinkle in flour and mix well with a whisk. Stir in milk, little by little, continuing to blend with flour. Mixture should be a thick pudding consistency. Add more milk or flour as needed to make a paste that pulls away from the sides of pan. Let cook 20 minutes slowly, adding milk when needed to keep it from getting too stiff. After 20 minutes, add in selected filling and mix well. Spread out and put on a plate. Let chill and become firm for 2 hours. Then, cut 2 x 1 inch sections, dredge in flour, then dip in beaten egg, then roll in bread crumbs. Fry quickly in hot oil, 2 minutes per side or until golden brown. Serves 4-6.

*Dora Ruíz Ortíz*

# MAIN
# DISHES

# Tender Beef Steak in Wine Sauce

*(Filete de Ternera en Salsa)*

2 lbs. choice beef steaks
5 cloves garlic, sliced
juice of 2 lemons
1 T. fresh parsley, snipped

2 tsp. salt
½ c. olive oil
1 c. white wine

Marinate steaks for at least 2 hours, but up to 24 hours, in marinade made of garlic, lemon juice, parsley and salt. After marinating, brown steaks one at a time in hot oil in heavy pot. Once all are browned, return all to pot with the wine. Let steaks simmer 10 minutes, then cover and simmer 20 minutes more. Place steaks on plates and drizzle a little of the pot broth over. Serves 4-6.

*Salud Borrego Méndez*

# Beef Stew

*(Caldereta)*

2 lbs. beef, cut up
¼ c. olive oil
1 onion, chopped
2 cloves garlic, minced
2 carrots, sliced
2 beef bouillon cubes
1 tsp. oregano

½ tsp. thyme
1 tsp. parsley
1 tsp. paprika
1 bay leaf
pinch pepper
salt to taste
½ c. white wine

Sear beef in hot oil in frying pan. Reduce heat to medium-high and add all ingredients except wine. Let cook for 10 minutes, stirring well. Reduce heat to medium-low and add wine. Cover pot if the wine evaporates before the meat is tender. Salt to taste. Serves 4-6.

*Lola Mesa Rodríguez*

# Hearty Potato Stew

*(Guiso de Patatas)*

¼ c. olive oil
4-5 cloves garlic
1 onion, chopped
2-3 carrots, sliced
½ lb. beef stew meat (or small
   beef or pork ribs)
1 tomato, chopped

¼ c. white wine
pinch black pepper
2 whole cloves
pinch saffron
2 chicken bouillon cubes
2-3 cups water
4-6 c. potatoes, quartered

Sauté garlic, onion and carrot in medium-hot oil, sautéing in that order. Add meat and stir. Add tomatoes and stir. Add rest of ingredients except potatoes, mixing well. Add enough water to cover. Let come to a boil on medium heat, then add potatoes. Boil gently until tender, around 40 minutes. Serves 4-6.

*Luisa Márquez Vázquez*

# Artichokes with Beef

*(Alcauciles)*

2 cloves garlic
1 onion
1 green pepper
1 tomato
2 carrots
1 bay leaf
olive oil for sautéing

½ lb. beef, cut up in pieces
   for stewing
salt
pepper
½ c. white wine
½ c. water
6 fresh artichokes

Chop first five ingredients. In order of listing, sauté one at a time in a little olive oil in a large saucepan, with the bay leaf. When finished, put all back in pan. Next, salt and pepper the meat and add to the sautéed vegetables. Brown meat, later adding wine and water. Let simmer 30-45 minutes. While the meat and vegetables cook, prepare artichokes. Remove the first two layers of leaves off the artichokes. Cut each across the middle, leaving a top half and a bottom half. Throw away the top half which is tough and bitter. Cut the remaining "heart" in quarters. Add to beef and vegetables. Stir. Let cook together 20 minutes. Serves 4.

*Dora Ruíz Ortíz*

# Fried Chicken Fillets

*(Filete de Pollo)*

2 cloves garlic, crushed
1 tsp. table salt
1 lb. chicken breast fillets
½-1 c. milk

1 egg, beaten
½ c. bread crumbs
½ c. olive oil

In a glass baking dish, put first the garlic bits and salt. Place fillets on top of garlic. Cover with milk. Cover dish and refrigerate 24 hours (turn fillets over half-way through). The next day, drain fillets. Dip each in a bowl containing the beaten egg, then dredge in bread crumbs. Fry in hot oil on both sides until meat tests done. Do not overcook. Frying time will depend on how thick the fillets are. Serves 4.

*Luisa Márquez Vázquez*

# Braised Garlic Chicken

*(Pollo al Ajillo)*

1 c. olive oil
2 bulbs garlic, each clove being peeled
4 lbs. chicken, bone-in, cut up in small
  pieces

1 c. white wine
salt and pepper

Lightly brown garlic cloves in a large frying pan in hot olive oil 2-3 minutes. Strain out garlic and put in a bowl, set aside. Fry chicken in same oil, browning only. Mash the garlic well and add wine to it, mixing well. Add this mix to the chicken. Let all simmer for 20 minutes. Do not cover. Add salt and pepper to taste. Serves 4-6.

*María Carmen Luque Martínez*

# Chicken á la King

*(Filete de Pollo con Nata)*

olive oil for frying
2 lbs. chicken fillets
2 eggs, beaten
bread crumbs
3 onions, chopped
6-oz. chopped turkey ham

6-oz. chopped cured ham
2 15-oz. cans sliced mushrooms
2½ c. light cream
3-4 slices mild cheese
salt
pepper

Dip fillets in beaten eggs, then dredge in bread crumbs. Fry in hot oil in frying pan until done. Drain fillets. Place in 11 x 13 inch baking dish. Set aside. In a deep frying pan, sauté onion, hams, and mushrooms together. Lower heat and add light cream, pepper and bouillon. Add cheese, let melt. Pour cream mixture over fillets. Put in oven to brown for 15 minutes on 350°. Serves 6.

*Adela Pineda Camino*

# Herbed Chicken

*(Pollo a las Finas Hierbas)*

2 T. olive oil
4 chicken leg quarters
2 c. water
1 T. butter
1 T. parsley, snipped

1 T. spring onion, chopped
1 T. thyme
½ c. crushed tomatoes
pinch pepper
½ c. cream

Sear chicken in frying pan. Add water and let simmer 20 minutes. Prepare herb sauce by melting butter in pan, adding in herbs and letting sauté for 2 minutes. Pour into pan with chicken; add tomatoes and pinch of pepper to chicken. Stir and let cook 5 minutes more. Add cream; heat while stirring. Blend well with spices. Serve chicken with sauce poured over. Serves 4.

*Adela Pineda Camino*

# Braised Chicken in Red Wine Sauce

*(Pollo al Vino Tinto)*

1 large onion, chopped
½ c. olive oil
6 chicken leg quarters

2 c. red wine
1 sm. hot chili pepper, chopped
salt to taste

Sauté chopped onion in hot oil in frying pan. Salt chicken as desired and place in sauté. Brown meat quickly, then add wine and hot pepper. Cover pan, let simmer until all wine is consumed. Serves 6.

*Joaquina Berengena García*

# Chicken Amandine

*(Pollo con Almendras)*

1 c. olive oil
1 whole chicken, cut up
4 oz. almonds, raw and peeled
2 carrots

1 onion, chopped
3-4 cloves garlic, whole
1 leek
1 c. white wine

Sear chicken quickly in hot oil, then set aside. In same pan, sauté first the almonds, then carrots, onion, garlic and leek, each individually. Remove each from oil and place in blender as soon as they are soft. Blend all at once, then put back in pan together with chicken. Stir in white wine, let simmer 10 minutes. Then cover pan and cook all slowly for one hour. Serves 4-6.

*Salud Borrego Méndez*

# Paula's Almond Chicken

*(Pollo con Almendras)*

½ c. olive oil
1 c. whole, raw almonds
1 bulb garlic, each clove peeled
1 slice crustless bread from
    baguette, crumbled

½ c. water
1 whole skinless chicken,
    cut-up
2 bay leaves
⅛ tsp. saffron

# Paula's Almond Chicken

## (Pollo con Almendras)

In frying pan, sauté almonds in hot oil until browned. Remove and set aside in a bowl. Sauté whole garlic cloves until soft. Remove and set aside with almonds. Fry bread crumbs until brown. Put in same bowl. Add water and toss. Pour all into a blender and purée. Set aside. Brown the chicken in remaining hot oil. When brown, remove any extra oil from pan. Pour purée on top of chicken. Add bay leaves and saffron. Simmer 10 minutes. Serves 4-6.

*Paula Pérez Benítez*

# Chicken and Shrimp Pasta

## (Tallarines con Pollo y Gambas)

| | |
|---|---|
| 1 boneless chicken breast | 12 oz. linguini pasta |
| ½ lb. shrimp, peeled | 2 oz. soy (or other bean) sprouts |
| 3 T. soy sauce, divided | 1 T. parsley flakes |
| 1 onion, chopped | 1 tsp. salt |
| 1 clove garlic, minced | |
| olive oil | |

Cut chicken into cubes and place in bowl together with the shrimp and 2 T. soy sauce. Let tenderize 5 minutes. Sauté onion and garlic in hot oil for 5 minutes in a large frying pan. Add in chicken and shrimp and cook 2-3 minutes more. Cook the pasta in boiling water until done. Drain and add to the frying pan, stirring well. Add in the soy sprouts, parsley, the remaining 1 T. of soy sauce and salt. Stir well. Serves 6-8.

*Sofía Mora*

# Turkey in Sauce

## (Pavo en Salsa)

| | |
|---|---|
| 1 turkey breast, cut up | 2 carrots, sliced |
| salt | 1 bay leaf |
| pepper | 1 c. white wine |
| 2 large onions, chopped | 2 chicken bouillon cubes |
| 1 whole garlic bulb, peeled | *(continued)* |

# Turkey in Sauce

## (Pavo en Salsa)

*(continued)* Sear salted and peppered turkey pieces. Take pieces out of pan and set aside. In the same pan, add oil, sauté the onions, carrots, bay leaf, and garlic, adding garlic last. Add white wine to sauté and bring all to boil. Once boiling, take pan off heat. Remove bay leaf. Transfer all vegetables to a blender and purée. Pour back into frying pan. Add in turkey pieces and let cool 15 minutes. Add water if the sauce gets too dry. Serves 4-6.

*Paula Pérez Benítez*


# Pork Fillets

## (Filete)

10 pork loin fillets, sliced thinly
olive oil for frying
3-4 cloves garlic, sliced

2 T. parsley, snipped
2 T. coarse salt
1 T. lemon juice

    Wash fillets under running water, dry. Heat oil in frying pan over medium-high heat and put 2-3 slices garlic in oil. Lay a fillet alongside and brown each side no more than 2-3 minutes. While it's frying, sprinkle with parsley, salt and lemon juice. Repeat for all fillets. Serves 4-6.

*Antonia Luque Martínez*


# Tenderloins á la Whiskey

## (Solomillo al Whiskey)

2 lbs. thin pork tenderloin fillets
coarse salt
olive oil for frying
10 cloves garlic, peeled
juice of one lemon

¼ c. whiskey or cognac
½ c. olive oil
¼ c. water
4 c. French fried potato
   wedges

    Salt fillets and brown quickly in a little oil in medium frying pan. Remove fillets and set aside. In same pan, heat ½ cup oil. Sauté garlic. Add lemon juice, whiskey and water.

# Tenderloins á la Whiskey

*(Solomillo al Whiskey)*

Let simmer 5 minutes. Lay fillets over a bed of hot French fried potato wedges and pour sauce over. Serves 6.

*Paula Pérez Benítez*

# Pork Tenderloin in Sherry Sauce

*(Cinta de Lomo en Salsa)*

½ c. olive oil
2 lbs. pork tenderloin
2 carrots, peeled and chopped

1 onion, chopped
1 large spring onion, sliced
1 c. sherry

Sauté meat and vegetables in olive oil over medium heat in a heavy pot. Stir frequently, turning meat as it browns. Once browned, cover pot and let simmer 1 hour. Afterwards, uncover pot and add sherry, letting it simmer uncovered 10 minutes. Cover once again, simmer 30 minutes. Remove vegetables from pot, put in blender and purée. Cut meat in slices and arrange on platter. Pour purée over meat. Serves 4-6.

*Salud Borrego Méndez*

# Pork in Wine Sauce

*(Cerdo en Salsa)*

½ c. olive oil
1 onion, chopped
1 Anaheim green pepper, chopped
1 large tomato, chopped
1 lb. pork, cut up

1 tsp. salt
1 bay leaf
2 whole peppercorns
½ c. white wine
6 boiled potatoes, chopped

Sauté onion, pepper and tomato in hot oil in a deep frying pan. Salt meat and add bay leaf to vegetables. Place meat on bottom of the pan and cover with sauté. Put peppercorns in wine and pour wine onto meat and vegetables. Simmer covered 45 minutes. In separate pot, boil potatoes. When all is tender, place potatoes on plate first and cover with meat and sauce. Serves 4-6.

*Tere Bernal*

# Oven-Baked Pork Tenderloin

*(Lomo al Horno)*

2 lbs. pork loins, sliced
1 c. red wine vinegar
1 T. oregano
4-5 cloves garlic, chopped

1½ tsp. black pepper
2 tsp. salt
1 egg white
2 T. sugar

Put loins in a flat casserole dish. Mix together vinegar, oregano, garlic, pepper and salt and pour over the loins. Let marinate 4-5 days in refrigerator. Then, in very cool place, hang loins in the air for 2 days to dry out, or else put between sheets of paper towels in the refrigerator for 2 days. Afterwards, place loins in clean baking dish and bake 45 minutes at 350°. When loins are done, beat the egg white and sugar together and brush it on the loins. Return meat to oven for 10 minutes. Serves 4-6.

*Joaquina Berengena García*

# Roasted Lamb

*(Cordero Asado)*

1 leg of lamb
1 large lemon
½ c. olive oil

2 T. bouillon granules
coarse salt

Clean leg of lamb well, removing extra fat. Lay in bottom of roasting pan. Prick entire leg with the point of a small knife 10 times on top, 10 on bottom. Halve the lemon and while squeezing, use both halves to rub over the leg. Brush on olive oil. Sprinkle bouillon granules over. Salt. Put in oven, covering lightly with aluminum foil. If possible, use only bottom element and bake at 350° for ½ hour. Remove lamb and flip top side down, baste with oil and pan drippings. Lightly recap with foil, and let cook ½ hour more. Remove foil, turn on top burner at 350° and let brown. Serves 4-6.

*Jonatán Gómez Martínez*

# Moroccan Lamb Stew

*(Guiso Marroquí de Cordero)*

2 lbs. lamb cuts  
½ c. olive oil  
1 onion, chopped  
1 turnip, chopped  
1 wedge cabbage, chopped  
2 carrots, sliced  
½ zucchini, chopped  
1 sm. wedge fresh pumpkin,  
    peeled and chopped  
½ eggplant, peeled and chopped  
2 c. cooked chickpeas  

water  
2 sprigs parsley and cilantro,  
    tied together  
½ tsp. turmeric  
½ tsp. curry powder  
½ tsp. cinnamon  
½ tsp. ginger  
½ tsp. saffron  
salt and pepper to taste  
6-8 c. cooked couscous  

    In a large, heavy stock pot, sear lamb pieces in olive oil until browned. Clean and chop or slice all vegetables until 1 inch chunk size. Add to meat. Stir in spices. Add water until it reaches half the level of the food. Bring to a boil, then simmer for 2 hours. Top the couscous with the meat and its sauce. Serves 6-8.

*Naciri Family*

# Grilled Lamb Chops

*(Cordero a la Brasa)*

2 lbs. lamb chops or ribs      coarse salt  
1 c. olive oil  

    Baste lamb with olive oil, sprinkle on salt and grill over hot charcoal fire, being careful not to overcook. As soon as the lamb is no longer pink in the center, it is done. Serves 4-6.

*Jonatán Gómez Martínez*

# Meatballs and Vegetables with Gravy

*(Albóndigas con Salsa)*

½ lb. ground pork
½ lb. ground beef
4 cloves garlic, minced, divided
1 onion, minced, divided
2 stalks parsley, snipped
¼-½ c. bread crumbs
1 egg
2 T. milk
⅔ c. white wine, divided

pinch black pepper
pinch ground cinnamon
1 tsp. salt
flour for breading
olive oil for frying
1 bay leaf
2 c. cooked peas
6 potatoes, cut in wedges
and fried

Mix meats, ½ of the minced garlic, ¼ of the minced onion, parsley, ¼ c. bread crumbs, egg, milk, 2 T. of white wine, pepper, cinnamon and salt until well blended. Add more breading crumbs if necessary to help meatballs hold together. Pinch off enough meat mixture to make 1 inch balls and roll each ball in breading flour. Drop in hot oil in frying pan. Turn to brown on all sides. Remove from pan and set aside. Make the gravy by sautéing the rest of the onion and garlic. When soft, put in bay leaf and rest of white wine, salting to taste. Add meatballs back into pan, simmering 15-20 minutes. Place green peas and French fries on each plate, laying the meat on top of the French fries. Pour sauce over all. Serves 4-6.

*Dora Ruíz Ortíz*

# Chickpea Stew

*(Cocido)*

1½ c. dried chickpeas, soaked
    overnight
2-3 c. recipe Consommé
2 oz. chorizo sausage
2-3 oz. salt pork with streaks of
    lean
½ lb. pork stew meat
¼ lb. pork rib pieces or soup
    bone
1 tsp. olive oil
1 carrot, in chunks
2 cloves garlic

1 onion, quartered
2 potatoes
1 tomato
1 red bell pepper, seeded
    and quartered
1 green bell pepper, seeded
    and quartered
½ leek
½ turnip
4 oz. fresh pumpkin, peeled
1 stalk celery without leaves

# Chickpea Stew

## (Cocido)

Put chickpeas in a large stock pot. Cover with Consommé. Pan-broil chorizo briefly to remove some fats. Set aside. Put all meats except sausage in with chickpeas. Stir in oil. Bring to boil, removing any foam that forms. Cover pot, letting cook over medium-low heat 40 minutes. Put in chorizo and all of vegetables. Let cook 20 minutes more, until all tender. Cut up any larger chunks of potatoes, celery, pumpkin, and turnips into smaller pieces. Serves 4-6.

*Luisa Márquez Vázquez*

# Chickpea Noodle Stew

## (Potaje de Garbanzos y Fideos)

2 qt. water
4-5 oz. dried chickpeas
4 oz. spinach
3 carrots
1 onion, chopped and divided
2 bay leaves

2 cloves garlic
2 T. flour
1 T. paprika
2 oz. fine short noodles
garnishes: chopped hard-
    boiled egg and minced
    parsley

Soak peas overnight. Clean spinach and carrots well. Put peas, spinach and carrots in a large pot with water. Add half the onion and the bay leaves. Bring to a boil and lower heat. Simmer 2 hours. Mince garlic and place it with the rest of the onion in a frying pan and sauté over low heat. Add flour to the sauté, stirring until blended. Stir in paprika. Pour sauté and noodles into stew and let cook 10 minutes more. Garnish with chopped egg and parsley. Serves 4-6.

*Adela Pineda Camino*

# Wrapped Franks

## (Salchichas Encapotadas)

1 lb. uncooked prepared pastry dough
10-12 thin frankfurters
Ketchup

mustard
beaten egg
*(continued)*

# Wrapped Franks

*(Salchichas Encapotadas)*

*(continued)* Roll out pastry dough large enough so that enough triangular pieces can be cut to wrap each frankfurter, each piece being approximately 6" x 6" x 6". Set frankfurters on one side of the pastry. Cutting lengthwise, slice halfway into the meat with a knife and into this opening squirt a line of ketchup and a line of mustard. Begin to roll meat up in the pastry, pulling side ends over as well and crimping the final tip back onto itself once rolled up. Set all on a greased baking tray and brush with beaten egg. Bake at 350° for 15 minutes. Serves 5-6.

*Tere Bernal*

# Cuban Rice

*(Arroz a la Cubana)*

¼ c. olive oil
10 cloves garlic, minced
2 chicken bouillon cubes
2 c. rice

4 c. water
16 oz. tomato sauce
4-6 eggs

　　Sauté garlic lightly in olive oil in a large frying pan. Add in rice, bouillon, and water. Bring to boil, then let simmer covered for 20 minutes. Heat tomato sauce separately once rice is almost done. Set aside. Fry one egg per person, set aside. On each individual plate, put a scooped mound of rice. Pour hot tomato sauce over and top with a fried egg. Serves 4-6.

*Pepi Titos González*

# Spanish Omelet

*(Tortilla)*

½ c. olive oil
2 lbs. peeled potatoes, thinly
　　sliced in rounds

1 onion, chopped fine
6 eggs
½ tsp. salt

# Spanish Omelet

## (Tortilla)

Heat oil in a medium-sized frying pan over medium heat. Put in potatoes and cover pan. Every minute or so, stir potatoes around. Do not let them get crispy. When potatoes begin to soften, add onions and stir. With the tip of the spatula, break potatoes into smaller pieces. Cover. Let cook 1-2 minutes more. While potatoes cook, beat eggs well in a bowl and add salt. Using a slotted spoon, remove potatoes and onions from pan and put into eggs. Stir all well. Take most of the remaining oil out of frying pan. Return pan to heat. Pour eggs and potato mixture back into frying pan. Reduce heat to low. Let omelet cook, covered, until edges begin to solidify and bottom is golden brown. Slide omelet onto a large plate, then flip upside down back into frying pan. Leave to cook 2-3 minutes more until golden brown. Remove from heat and serve. Serves 6.

*Joaquina Berengena García*

# Potato Omelet with Garlic

## (Tortilla con Ajo)

| | |
|---|---|
| 1 c. olive oil | 2 cloves garlic, minced |
| 2 lbs. potatoes, peeled and sliced thinly | 4-5 eggs, beaten |

In medium non-stick frying pan, heat oil. Sauté potatoes, breaking into pieces as they soften. As they become soft but not yet crispy, add in garlic. Let sauté for 2 minutes more, then strain potatoes and garlic out of oil and put in a bowl. Drain off almost all of the oil out of pan. Pour beaten eggs over potatoes, turn to coat all. Pour this back into hot pan. Cover, and let cook in low for 10-15 minutes, until tortilla is almost set and golden brown. Putting a large plate on top of the frying pan, invert pan and plate so that tortilla is now on the plate. Add 1 T. of oil back to pan, and quickly slide tortilla back into pan, uncooked side down. Let cook 2 minutes more. Remove from heat. Turn tortilla out onto a plate and let cool slightly. Serves 6-8.

*Paula Pérez Benítez*

# Ham Tortilla

---

*(Tortilla de Jamón)*

½ c. olive oil                    3-4 eggs, beaten
1 c. cured ham, shredded         ½ tsp. black pepper

Sauté ham for 1 minute over medium heat in a medium-sized non-stick frying pan. Mix eggs and black pepper and pour into frying pan. Turn to low heat. Let cook slowly until eggs begin to set all the way through. With a wooden spoon, beginning at one side of the tortilla, begin rolling tortilla up. If it needs further cooking, let it sit in the hot pan, covered, with the burner turned off, for 1-2 minutes more. Serves 3-4.

*Salud Borrego Méndez*


# Asparagus and Ham Mix-Up

---

*(Revuelto de Espárrago con Jamón)*

1 lb. fresh asparagus             cured ham, cubed
1 clove garlic, minced            2 eggs
olive oil

Cut up asparagus and boil in a saucepan until tender crisp. Drain and set aside. Sauté garlic in oil in a frying pan until soft. Stir in ham cubes and cook 5 minutes. Add in drained asparagus and stir well. Crack 2 eggs over the pan and mix in, coating asparagus well. Serves 4.

*Rosa Garrido Serrano*


# Seafood Paella

---

*(Paella Marinera)*

½ c. olive oil                    1 bay leaf
1 T. parsley, minced              4¼ c. water
1 red bell pepper, seeded and     4 oz. squid, sliced in rings
   chopped          6 oz. fresh clams in the shell

# Seafood Paella

*(Paella Marinera)*

1 green bell pepper, seeded and chopped
1 large tomato, diced
2 cloves garlic, minced
2 c. uncooked short-grain rice

4 oz. mild white fish, deboned
8 oz. mixture, of small, medium and large shrimp, whole
1 T. salt
⅛ tsp. saffron

In a wide, flat frying pan on an equal sized burner, heat oil and sauté the parsley, peppers and tomato until soft. Add garlic the last minute, stirring well. Add the rice and bay leaf to the sauté along with the shrimp and other seafood. Add water. Stir in salt and saffron, mixing well into water. Let all come to a boil, then simmer covered for 20-30 minutes until rice is tender. Drizzle more olive oil over all. Serves 4-6.

*María José Guerrero Abril*


# Andalucían Paella

*(Paella Andaluza)*

½ lb. seafood in the shell (clams, shrimp, mussels)
1 lb. chicken, cut up in small pieces
½ lb. pork roast, cut up in small pieces
1 clove garlic
½ onion
1 T. dried parsley

2 large tomatoes
1 red bell pepper
1 green bell pepper
½ c. olive oil
1 T. salt
2 c. uncooked short grain rice
¼ c. white wine
4½ c. water
⅛ tsp. saffron

Clean seafood and set aside. In a wide flat frying pan on an equal size burner, heat oil and fry meats (not seafood) until brown. Remove meats and set aside. Clean and finely chop all vegetables. Sauté them in the same frying pan until soft, but not browned. Put meats and seafood in with vegetables, and add salt, rice and white wine. Stir well. Pour water into pan and stir gently. Cover and cook 20-30 minutes until rice is tender. Serves 4-6.

*Joaquina Berengena García*

# Fish Fillets a la Roteña

*(Urta a la Roteña)*

¼ c. olive oil
1 red bell pepper, julienne
1 green bell pepper, julienne
1 onion, julienne
4 ripe tomatoes, peeled and crushed

salt
pepper
2 lbs. amberjack fillets

Sauté the peppers and onion in hot oil until soft. Stir in tomatoes, salt and pepper to taste. Let simmer and thicken 5 minutes. Remove sauté to bowl. Lay fish in frying pan on top of remaining oil and brown quickly. Remove and place in baking dish. Put vegetable sauté over the top of fish and bake at 350° for 5-10 minutes until fish is flaky. Serves 4-6.

*Salud Borrego Méndez*


# Mediterranean Sword Fish

*(Pez Espada)*

¼ c. olive oil
2 lbs. swordfish, whole or filleted
2 cloves garlic, minced
1 stalk parsley, snipped

salt
pepper
4-6 lemon halves

In frying pan, heat oil and place fish in the pan, being careful not to overlap edges. Sauté garlic and parsley alongside fish. Let fish cook over medium-high heat, turning after 2-4 minutes, depending on thickness of fish. Once done (fish will flake when pierced with a fork), arrange on plates with a lemon half beside each fish to squeeze over just before eating. Serves 4-6.

*Paula Pérez Benítez*

# Joaquina's Hake

*(Merluza)*

olive oil

1 onion, chopped

2 T. flour

½ c. water

2 lbs. hake or other mild white
   fish, filleted

2 stalks parsley, snipped

1 T. lemon juice

salt

Pour oil in frying pan to 1 inch deep.  Add onion, sauté well.  Add flour, stir until it thickens.  Add water, then lay fish fillets in the pan.  Sprinkle parsley over.  Drizzle with lemon. Let boil 5-10 minutes, till fish flakes.  Salt and serve.  Serves 4-6.

*Joaquina Berengena García*


# Hake Sauté

*(Merluza)*

2 large onions, diced

1 tomato peeled, and halved if large

1 green bell pepper, seeded and quartered

2 lbs. hake (or mild white fish)

salt

lemon

¼ c. olive oil

Sauté vegetables in oil. When tender, add in fish and cook 5 minutes. Salt, and squeeze lemon juice over. Serves 4.

*Carmen del Bot*


# Salt Encrusted Baked Fish (or Chicken)

*(Pescado o Pollo a la Sal)*

1-2 lbs. coarse salt

2-3 whole fish or 1 whole chicken

On a baking sheet with low edges, pour a thin, but solid layer of the coarse salt. Place fish or chicken on top. By the handful, place more salt generously on top of the meat, packing it down well to completely encase the meat. It will look like a white mound. The salt will form a crust as the meat bakes.

*(continued)*

# Salt Encrusted Baked Fish (or Chicken)

*(Pescado o Pollo a la Sal)*

*(continued)* Bake in a 350 degree oven, allowing 15 minutes/pound for fish; 30 minutes/pound for the chicken. A small portion of the salt crust may be removed to test for doneness. (When done, fish meat will flake at its thickest part, and chicken will not ooze pink juices when pierced with a fork at a thick part.) Remove from oven, and remove salt crust entirely. Brush off stray pieces of salt if desired. Meat will be tender and juicy.

*Alonso Hidalgo and Lourdes Cotta*

# Basque Hake

*(Merluza a la Vasca)*

¾ c. olive oil
6 cloves garlic, sliced
6 large, round slices of hake
salt
1 egg, beaten

½ lb. black clams
½ lb. shrimp
1 c. white wine
1 branch parsley
1 loaf hard bread

Sauté garlic in oil in frying pan until soft. Remove garlic and set aside. Sprinkle salt on fish, dip in beaten egg and fry lightly on both sides. Do several slices at a time, being careful to not put one on top of another. Once done, move slices to a new frying pan. Lay garlic slices on top of fish. Put unopened clams and peeled shrimp on top of garlic. Pour the used oil, white wine and parsley over all. Let come to boil uncovered. Salt if needed. When clams open and fish is just flaky, pull bread apart in chunks and place in sauce. Serves 6.

*María Carmen Luque Martínez*

# Radio Genesis Fish Casserole

*(Pescado Radio Génesis)*

6 fish fillets
2 lbs. small potatoes, peeled
2 tomatoes, chopped
1 green bell pepper, chopped
2 cloves garlic, minced

½ onion, chopped
½ c. olive oil
fresh parsley sprigs
¼ c. white wine
salt to taste

In large frying pan, pour olive oil and sauté tomatoes, pepper, garlic and onion until soft. Strain from the oil and set aside. Slice peeled potatoes in rounds ½ inch thick. Salt them and then fry in leftover oil until soft but not crispy. Remove from oil. Place potatoes in a 9 x 13 inch baking pan. Put raw fish on top of potatoes. Salt. Spread the sautéed vegetables over the fish. Snip parsley and sprinkle over. Pour wine over all. Bake at 350° for 20 minutes until fish is flaky. Serves 6.

*María Carmen Luque Martínez*


# Marinated Dogfish (Shark)

*(Adobo)*

1 lb. dogfish (shark)
1 whole bulb garlic, peeled and
   mashed in mortar
2 T. oregano
4 T. red wine vinegar

½ tsp. paprika
1½ T. salt
water
flour

Lay fish in a glass or ceramic platter with sides. Make a dressing of the rest of the ingredients, adding water to make about 1 cup total. Pour over fish and let marinate in refrigerator for 24 hours. The next day, drain off liquid. Cut fish in 1 inch squares, dredge in flour for frying and then fry quickly in hot oil until flaky. Serves 4-6.

*María Carmen Luque Martínez*

# Fried Squid

*(Calamares Fritos)*

1 lb. sliced small squid        vegetable oil for deep fat frying
flour for breading            salt

Cut seafood in ¼ inch rings. Dredge in flour. Fry in hot oil till lightly browned. Drain and salt. Serves 4.

*Carmen del Bot*

# Potatoes and Squid

*(Papas con Choco)*

2 cloves garlic              ½ c. white wine
1 onion, chopped         ½ c. water
1 Anaheim green pepper, chopped    pinch saffron
1 tomato, diced              4 potatoes, peeled and
1 carrot, chopped              quartered
1 lb. large squid, cut up into chunks

In order, sauté individually the garlic, onion, pepper, tomato, carrot, setting each aside once soft. Add all back to pan, mixing in the squid chunks as well. Add wine, water and saffron and let simmer 5 minutes. Add in potatoes and let cook 10-15 minutes with pan lid half open. Serves 4-6.

*Dora Ruíz Ortíz*

# Herbed Squid

*(Calamares al Perejil)*

1½-2 lbs. small squid        1 parsley branch
4 lemons, divided           salt
4 cloves garlic (1 whole, 3 chopped)    lettuce leaves
2 T. olive oil

Clean squid and cook in salted water to cover with the juice of 2 lemons and the whole garlic clove for 15-20 minutes. Make a sauce from the juice of 2 lemons, oil, parsley and chopped garlic. Spread lettuce leaves on a platter. Arrange whole squid on top of lettuce. Drizzle with lemon sauce. Serves 6-8.

*Adela Pineda Camino*

# Roasted Sardines

*(Sardinas Asadas)*

8-12 fresh sardines                    coarse salt
olive oil

    Clean sardines. Baste with olive oil and sprinkle on salt. Bake in oven at 325° for 20 minutes. Serves 4-6.

*Dora Ruíz Ortíz*


# Adela's Favorite Fish Stew

*(Caldereta de Pescado)*

1 c. olive oil                         ¾ lb. fish
1 onion, chopped                       1 T. paprika
½ green bell pepper, chopped           1 T. saffron
4 tomatoes, chopped                    1 stalk parsley, minced
4 potatoes, peeled and thinly sliced   1 bouillon cube
½-1 c. water                           pinch black pepper

    In a deep frying pan, sauté in hot oil the onion, bell peppers and tomatoes. Add potatoes and ½ c. water. Bring to boil. Add fish and all other ingredients. Simmer 15 minutes. Do not let boil dry. Serves 4-6.

*Adela Pineda Camino*


# Cod with Chickpeas

*(Garbanzos con Bacalao)*

1 lb. chickpeas, soaked overnight      4 cloves garlic, minced
3 c. recipe for Consommé               1 c. olive oil
1 green bell pepper, chopped           ½ lb. cod
1 tomato, diced                        pinch saffron
2 potatoes, diced                      1 bay leaf
1 onion, chopped

    Boil chickpeas 2 hours until soft in consommé. Sauté vegetables, adding garlic last. Add cleaned cod and bay leaf. Let cook until cod is flaky. Strain cod out of oil and add to pot of chickpeas. Simmer 15 minutes. Serve hot. Serves 4-6.

*Carmen del Bot*

# Tuna Fish Pie

(Empanada de Atún)

2 unbaked pastry sheets,
  about 11 x 15 inches each
⅓ c. olive oil
salt
1 onion sliced in strips
2 green bell peppers

16 oz. crushed tomato
1 lb. tuna, drained
⅛ tsp. black pepper
1 tsp. oregano
2 eggs, beaten
4-5 cloves garlic, sliced

Spread out one pastry sheet on a flat baking tray. Sauté onion, peppers and garlic together in oil in a large frying pan. Salt to taste. Add crushed tomato, let simmer 20 minutes. Put in tuna, sprinkle in pepper and oregano, stirring well into vegetables. Spread this mixture out over pastry, leaving edges dry. Put other pastry sheet on top. Crimp edges of the two pastries together. Brush egg on top of pastry. If desired, pastry can be scored with a knife. Bake at 350° for 20 minutes or until golden brown. Serves 6.

*Paula Pérez Benítez*

*Photograph courtesy of Rich Milne*

# BREADS

# &

# ROLLS

# Spanish Breakfast Toast for Adults

*(Tostada para Adultos)*

1 large dense bun or rustic
  bread with soft white crust
olive oil, to taste

coarse salt, to taste
garnishes: thin cured ham
  slices, tomato slices, garlic

Halve bun. Toast the top half of each. Drizzle on olive oil and sprinkle on salt. Top with any or all of the garnishes. Serves 1.

*Encarni Domínguez Ledesma*


# Spanish Breakfast Toast for Kids

*(Tostada para Niños)*

1 large dense bun or rustic
  bread with soft white crust
olive oil and sugar

margarine and jam

Halve bun. Toast the top half of each. Either drizzle on olive oil and sprinkle on sugar; or spread on margarine and jam. Serves 1.

*Encarni Domínguez Ledesma*


# Bread of the House

*(Pan de la Casa)*

1 baguette
1-2 cups recipe Eduardo's Summer Soup

4-6 oz. cured ham
½ c. olive oil

Slice bread in half length-wise, cut in sections, and toast in oven. Spread soup over the sections of bread. Place thin ham slices on top. Drizzle with olive oil.

*Eduardo Pérez González*

# Breakfast Muffins

*(Magdalenas)*

6 eggs
1½ c. sugar
1½ c. olive oil

2½ c. flour
4 tsp. baking powder
1 tsp. salt

Beat the eggs together with the sugar and oil. Add the flour, baking powder and salt and continue to mix until all is well blended. Bake in greased muffin tins at 350° for 15-20 minutes. Makes 1½ dozen.

*Susana Ruíz Pérez*

# Chocolate Muffins

*(Magdalenas de Chocolate)*

2 eggs, beaten
1 c. whole milk
¼ c. vegetable oil
1½ c. flour
1 tsp. baking powder

1 tsp. salt
½ c. sugar
7 oz. sweetened baking
   chocolate, grated

In a bowl, mix eggs, milk and oil. Add dry ingredients, mix well. Finally, stir in grated chocolate. Grease a muffin tin and fill ¾ full with batter. Bake at 350° for 20-25 minutes until test done. Makes 1 dozen.

*Antonia Luque Martínez*

# Sunday Morning Churros Pastries

*(Churros)*

1 c. all-purpose flour
1 c. water
pinch salt

1½ qt. oil
confectioner's sugar
1 recipe Hot Chocolate for Churros

*(continued)*

# Sunday Morning Churros Pastries

*(Churros)*

*(continued)* Mix water and salt. Heat water in a medium pot. When boiling, add flour, stirring well with a wooden spoon until all blended and begins to hold together in a lump. Remove from heat, let cool some. Heat oil to 375 degrees in a deep fat fryer or heavy pot. Filling a pastry sleeve or soft funnel with the dough, squeeze dough in a spiral into the oil. Cover loosely to avoid splatters. Let brown on one side, flip using a long spatula, and brown on the other. Take churro out, let drain, and cut with scissors. Sprinkle confectioner's sugar over or dip pastries into Hot Chocolate. Makes 4 servings.

*María Carmen Luque Martínez*

# Hot Gypsy Crullers

*(Buñuelos de los Gitanos)*

4½-5½ c. all purpose flour
1 pkt. dry yeast
1 T. sugar
1 tsp. salt
½ tsp. baking soda
1 c. water

1 c. milk
frying oil (not olive oil)
garnishes: Hot Chocolate for
    Churros, sugar, honey or
    cinnamon

Mix dry ingredients beginning with 4½ c. flour, yeast, sugar, salt and soda. Add in milk and enough water to make a soft dough. Dough should be sticky and almost runny. Set aside in a warm place to let rise until doubled in size. Once dough has finished rising, begin heating oil to 375° in a heavy pan or fryer. Using a pastry sleeve, squeeze dough into heated oil, making 2 inch round circles. Fry about 1 minute on each side, or until golden. Top with a garnish and/or dip in Hot Chocolate drink. Serves 6.

*Carmen del Bot*

# Moroccan Bread

*(Pan Marroquí)*

4-5 c. all-purpose flour
1½ tsp. salt

1 pkg. yeast
1-1¼ c. warm water

Mix dry ingredients well. Add water until dough forms a ball, stirring with wooden spoon until well-mixed. Turn out onto floured surface and knead well for 10 full minutes. Let rest 10 minutes. Flatten on a lightly greased pizza pan or large cookie sheet into a round wheel. Let sit covered in a warm place until risen to 1 inch high. Bake at 375° until lightly browned. Cut in wedges and serve. Serves 6-8.

*Naciri Family*

# Holy Week French Toast

*(Semana Santa Torrijas)*

12 oz. sliced loaf of dense white bread
1 c. water, divided
2 c. white wine

1 c. honey
6 eggs
1-2 c. frying oil

Mix ½ c. water with wine in bowl. Beat eggs in another bowl. Heat ½ c. oil in a large frying pan. Mix honey with ½ c. water in a pot and heat through. Take one slice of bread and dip it quickly in the water/ wine, then coat it in egg, then fry both sides in hot oil. When golden, remove slice and dip in honey/water. Place on platter and cut in one inch strips. Keep honey just below boiling point. Continue dipping all slices of bread in this manner, adding oil to frying pan as necessary. Serves 10-12.

*Tere Bernal*

# Tropical Bread

---

*(Pan Tropical)*

6-10 bread rolls, toasted
16 oz. tuna in olive oil
1 onion, minced fine
15 oz. crushed tomato
1 tsp. salt
1 T. oregano

1 T. vinegar
1 small red hot chili pepper
¼ tsp. cumin
¼ tsp. cilantro
¼ tsp. black pepper
¼ tsp. ground cloves

    In a frying pan, put in tuna with oil and onion, mixing well. Stir in crushed tomato, salt, oregano and vinegar. Mix all over low heat for 10 minutes. Let cool. Open hot rolls and spread filling inside. Serves 4-6.

*Lola Mesa Rodríguez*

# Bread with Codfish Spread

---

*(Pan de Bacalao)*

10-12 slices bread
1 c. recipe for Eduardo's
  Summer Soup

8 oz. smoked cod, in strips
2 T. parsley, minced

    Toast bread slices, spread on Eduardo's Summer Soup and lay codfish strips on top. Sprinkle parsley over. Serves 4-6.

*Lola Mesa Rodríguez*

# DESSERTS

# Classic Flan

*(Flan Clásico)*

½ c. sugar (for caramel)
7 eggs
1 lg. can (24 oz.) sweetened
   condensed milk

1 can fresh whole milk (using
   empty condensed milk can
   to measure)
1 tsp. vanilla

    Melt ½ c. sugar in a heavy frying pan over medium heat, stirring until brown and syrupy but not burnt. Pour into individual custard cups or one 2 qt. baking dish immediately after syrup is ready, coating the sides and bottom. Caramel will harden quickly. Beat eggs and milks together until well blended. Pour on top of caramel. Place baking dish into a 9 x 13 inch baking dish (or larger) that is half-filled with hot water. Place in middle of oven and bake at 350°, checking to see if done after 45 minutes. Flan is done when the center is set and firm to touch. Chill. The flan can either be scooped directly out of the dish with the caramel sauce spooned over, or invert the bowl on a platter after first briefly warming the bowl in a little hot water. For individual servings, custard cups should be filled with first the hot caramel syrup, then the flan mixture and lastly baked in the water bath. Serves 6-8.

*Tere Bernal*

# Eduardo's Egg Custard

*(Flan de Huevo)*

*Caramel Topping*

½ c. sugar

    Stir sugar in a medium hot frying pan until all crystals liquefy into syrup. Do not let burn. Pour at once into 6 custard cups or into one 2-quart baking dish, coating bottom completely.

*Custard*

10 egg yolks
1 c. sugar

2 c. whole milk

# Eduardo's Egg Custard

*(Flan de Huevo)*

Beat the 10 yolks, slowly adding in the sugar and milk. When all blended, fill the custard cups (or baking dish), pouring on top of caramel. Set cups or baking dish in a hot water bath and bake in the oven at 400° for 40 minutes, using only the bottom element. If both elements must be used, bake at 350° until set, around 1 hour, depending on size of cups or dish. Serves 6.

*Eduardo Pérez González*

# Heavenly Custard

*(Tocino del Cielo)*

| | |
|---|---|
| 1 c. sugar (for caramel) | ½ c. sugar |
| 7 egg yolks | 1 c. water |

Make caramel and pour in the bottom of the baking dish, following the directions for Classic Flan. Mix egg yolks with ½ c. sugar until foamy, add water, mixing well. Pour into the caramelized 9 x 9 inch baking dish and baking the custard as for the Classic Flan. Serves 4-6.

*Carmen del Bot*

# Vanilla Cream Pudding

*(Natillas)*

| | |
|---|---|
| 3 T. cornstarch | 1 lemon rind |
| 6 c. whole milk | ½ tsp. vanilla |
| 6 egg yolks, beaten | ½ tsp. cinnamon |
| 6 T. sugar | vanilla wafers |

In large saucepan, completely dissolve cornstarch in ½ c. of the cold milk. Add the rest of the milk, egg yolks, sugar, lemon rind (with interior white pith peeled off) and ½ tsp. vanilla. Blend well with wire whisk. Heat over medium heat, stirring constantly until mixture thickens, then cook 2 minutes more. Remove from heat. Remove lemon rind. Pour into large shallow bowl or 8 shallow dessert bowls and sprinkle a little cinnamon over. Place vanilla wafers on top. Chill well. Serves 6-8.

*Tere Bernal*

# Chocolate Mousse

---

### (Mousse de Chocolate)

3 eggs, separated  
1 c. melted milk chocolate  
2 T. water

3 T. sugar  
6 oz. whipped cream

In mixer, whip egg whites, set aside. To the melted chocolate, blend in water. With mixer, beat egg yolks with sugar until creamy. Add the melted chocolate, mix well. Fold in whipped cream and egg whites until smooth. Fill in individual dessert cups and let chill 2 hours. Serves 4.

*Carmen del Bot*

# Lemon Mousse

---

### *(Mousse de Limón)*

2 c. whipping cream  
12 oz. sweetened condensed milk

1 c. lemon juice

Chill mixing bowl and cream in freezer for 30 minutes. Remove bowl from freezer and pour cream in. Whip cream until very stiff. Fold in the milk and juice by hand, folding carefully for just a few seconds. Pour into individual dessert cups and refrigerate until ready to serve. Serves 6-8.

*Susana Ruíz Pérez*

# Stirred Dessert

---

### (Poleá)

½ - ¾ cup olive oil  
2 slices of dense white bread, crumbled  
   in small bits  
1 whole lemon peel, cut into 6-8 pieces  
2 tsps. anise seed

1 stick cinnamon  
6 Tbsp. flour  
3 cups milk  
6 Tbsp. sugar  
Ground cinnamon

# Stirred Dessert

(Poleá)

In a medium, heavy frying pan, heat ½ cup oil over medium high heat. Place bread bits in hot oil and fry, stirring often, until golden brown. Strain bread out of oil and set to one side. In the same oil, fry lemon peel until brown. Remove and discard. Lower heat to medium low. Fry anise and cinnamon stick in the oil for 1-2 minutes, then strain out the anise and discard, but set the cinnamon aside. Then slowly whisk flour into oil (add more oil if needed), mixing until no lumps are visible. Slowly pour in milk, stirring continuously until blended and creamy. Add sugar, and stir. Add cinnamon stick back in. Bring mixture to a slow bubbling state and maintain while it thickens. Let cook for 20 minutes, stirring frequently to keep it from burning and adding more milk if pudding thickens too much (it should still be able to pour off a spoon). Remove the cinnamon stick and discard. Pour the pudding into 6-8 small dessert bowls. Sprinkle the bread bits over each pudding. Sprinkle ground cinnamon over top of bread. Serve while bread is still crispy.

*From several friends*

# Chilled Cinnamon Cream

*(Crema Fría de Canela)*

4 c. milk, divided
4 T. sugar
1 stick cinnamon

4 egg yolks
1 c. plain yogurt

In saucepan, heat 3 cups of milk with sugar and cinnamon stick. Let simmer 10 minutes. In separate bowl, beat egg yolks. Add in other 1 cup of milk and beat. Pour egg/milk mixture into saucepan. Stir well. On medium heat, stir gently until thickened, about 4 minutes. Remove cinnamon stick. Let milk mixture cool. Add the yogurt, blending well. Pour into 6-8 shallow custard cups. Sprinkle with ground cinnamon. Serves 6.

*Tere Bernal*

# Rice Pudding

*(Arroz con Leche)*

2 c. water  
1½ c. rice  
1 qt. milk  
⅔ c. sugar

¼ tsp. vanilla  
Zest of 1 lemon  
2 cinnamon sticks  
ground cinnamon to garnish

In one saucepan, bring rice to boil, then simmer, in water for 8 minutes. In another saucepan, heat milk, and sugar with vanilla, lemon zest and cinnamon stick. After rice cooks 8 minutes, strain out any remaining water and add rice to hot milk. Stir with wooden spoon from time to time, leaving to simmer for 15 minutes. Remove lemon zest and cinnamon sticks. Pour into individual bowls and sprinkle with ground cinnamon. Chill 2-3 hours. Serves 4-6.

*Tere Bernal*

# Christmas Pastries

*(Pestiños)*

½ c. olive oil  
the rind of ½ lemon, with pith  
   removed  
½ tsp. anise seed, crushed  
¼ c. white wine

2 ½ - 3 c. all-purpose flour  
2 c. frying oil  
½ c. honey  
2 T. water

Heat oil in frying pan until hot, and put in lemon rind and fry. When golden, take pan off heat, remove rind and put in anise seed. Let oil cool. In a stoneware bowl, pour the oil into the wine. Add flour ½ c. at a time and stir well with a fork. Keep adding flour until a fairly dry dough, such as a pie crust, is formed. On a floured surface, roll out dough very thin as for a pie crust and cut in 4 inch squares. Heat frying oil in frying pan. Take each dough square and pull together the two opposite corners and pinch in order to form a "bow-tie." Fry in deep hot oil until golden. Heat honey with water until syrupy. Dip each pastry in syrup, and lay on a plate to cool. Repeat with all dough squares. Makes 1-2 dozen.

*Salud Borrego Méndez*

# Christmas Shortbread

## (Mantecados)

1 c. butter or vegetable shortening (not margarine)
1 c. confectioner's sugar
¾ c. toasted almonds, chopped

2½ - 3 c. flour
1 egg
garnishes: sesame seed, confectioner's sugar

In order listed, mix first four ingredients by hand in a big bowl until crumbly. Add enough flour to make a dough that holds its shape and is not sticky. On a cool surface, roll dough out flat to 1 inch thick. Using a small cookie cutter, make cut outs. Place on a greased baking sheet. Beat egg and brush on top. Bake in oven for 15 minutes at 350°, or until lightly browned. Serves 4-6.

*Paula Pérez Benítez*

# Chocolate "Salami"

## (Salchichón de Chocolate)

16 oz. baking chocolate
8 oz. confectioner's sugar
8 oz. softened regular margarine or butter

2 eggs
4 c. vanilla wafers or graham crackers
1 T. cognac

Melt chocolate slowly in a double boiler or in the microwave. In a mixing bowl, mix the chocolate, sugar, margarine and eggs until creamy and fluffy. Break wafers into small pieces and stir into chocolate mixture. On a large piece of wax paper, turn mixture out and brush it with cognac. Roll mixture up in a log 2 inches wide and seal paper. Place in refrigerator until hardened. Later, remove paper and slice thinly as for salami. Makes 1 log.

*María José Guerrero Abril*

# Grandma's Dessert

### (El Postre de la Abuela)

8 oz. vanilla wafers  
3-4 oz. walnut meats  
2 oz. hazelnut meats  

2 oz. almonds  
1 c. whipping cream  

Crush wafers until almost powdery. Finely chop the nuts. Mix well with the wafers. Whip the cream until stiff peaks form. Gently fold nut/wafer mix into cream, and blend well. Place mix on a sheet of aluminum foil and roll up into a log 1-2 inches thick. Seal well and refrigerate. To eat, slice off rounds and refrigerate remaining log. Makes 1 log.

*Susana Ruíz Pérez*

# Chocolate Truffles

### (Trufas)

1 c. unsalted margarine or butter  
3 egg yolks  
6 T. sweetened condensed milk  
1 oz. cognac  

8 oz. cocoa  
chocolate sprinkles  
paper candy cups  

Soften margarine. Add to a bowl with the egg yolks and mix. Blend in milk, cognac and cocoa. Mash well with a fork. Let chill in refrigerator 2-3 hours. Later, take spoonfuls of the candy and roll into a ball. Put chocolate sprinkles in a bowl, and roll the balls in the sprinkles until coated. Set in little candy papers and let chill again in refrigerator until ready to serve.

*Antonia Luque Martínez*

# Fried Milk Squares

### (Leche Frita)

1 qt. milk  
4 T. flour  
9 T. sugar  
1 lemon rind  
2 sticks cinnamon  

2 eggs, beaten  
bread crumbs for breading  
1 ½ c. salad oil  
½ tsp. cinnamon for sprinkling  
½ c. sugar for sprinkling

# Fried Milk Squares

*(Leche Frita)*

In small bowl blend together 1 c. milk and the flour. Set aside. Put the other 3 c. milk in a pot with the 9 T. sugar, lemon rind and cinnamon sticks. Heat this until it comes to a boil. Remove lemon rind. Add in milk and flour mix. Keep stirring over low heat until the dough forms a mass that pulls away from pan. Spread dough onto a long tray one inch thick. Let cool. Cut in small squares. Dip each square in the beaten eggs, then in bread crumbs. Fry in hot oil. Drain each. Sprinkle with cinnamon sugar. Makes approximately 12-15 squares.

*Tere Bernal*

# Almond Torte

*(Tarta de Almendra)*

| | |
|---|---|
| 1 ½ c. sugar (divided) | 4 eggs |
| 1 c. raw almonds | 2 c. milk |
| 15 vanilla wafers | |

Put ½ cup sugar in a heavy frying pan over medium heat. Stirring sugar constantly, let it melt into a thick brown caramel syrup. As soon as all crystals are melted, pour into a 2 qt. rounded baking dish, coating the entire bottom. Let cool. In a blender, purée the remaining 1 c. sugar, the almonds, vanilla wafers and eggs until no nuts or crumbs are visible. Add in milk and blend well to mix. Pour this into the caramelized bowl. Bake in oven at 350° for 30 minutes or until set. Serves 6-8.

Carmen del Bot

# Spanish Tiramisú

*(Tiramisú Española)*

| | |
|---|---|
| 2 quarts heavy whipping cream, chilled | 1 cup strong coffee |
| 1 ¼ cup sugar | Soft thick vanilla cookies |
| 8 oz. cream cheese or mascarpone cheese | Cocoa drink mix powder |

*(continued)*

# Spanish Tiramisú

## (Tiramisú Española)

*(continued)* Whip cream and sugar together until thick. Slowly add cheese, beating into a creamy paste in bowl. In an oblong pan, dip cookies in coffee and place in a layer on bottom. Spread whipped cream paste over cookies. Sprinkle cocoa powder on top of cream. Repeat layers until cake is as high as wished. Refrigerate 12-24 hours before serving.

*María del Carmen Navarro García*


# Gypsy Arm Jelly Roll

## (Brazo de Gitano)

*Cream Filling*

| | |
|---|---|
| 2 c. milk | 2 T. cornstarch |
| 1 tsp. lemon zest, white pith removed | ⅓ c. milk |
| 1 tsp. vanilla | 2 ½ T. butter |
| 3 egg yolks | |

Bring milk to a boil with lemon zest in a small saucepan. Take off heat, let cool. Stir in vanilla. Remove lemon. Mix egg yolks, cornstarch and sugar in a bowl. Add milk to yolks and beat well. Pour mixture all back in pot and bring just to boil. Take off heat, melt in butter. Set aside and let cool.

*Prepare Cake*

| | |
|---|---|
| 5 eggs, separated | ¾ c. flour |
| ¾ c. sugar | topping: confectioner's sugar and |
| 1 T. lemon zest | cinnamon, or chocolate icing |

In a bowl, whip egg whites until stiff. Set aside. In another bowl, mix the egg yolks with the sugar and lemon zest until creamy. Add flour slowly. Fold egg whites into batter. Line a 15 x 20 inch baking pan with wax paper. Grease and flour sides of pan. Spread batter into pan using a spatula. Bake at 350° for 10 minutes. Remove cake with paper intact and set on a counter. Let cool 5 minutes. Spread cream filling over the cake. Roll up as a jelly roll, removing paper at the same time. Once rolled, wrap paper around cake to hold it tightly in place. Let cool. Remove paper. Sprinkle cake with the topping. Slice in rounds. Serves 6-8.

*Tere Bernal*

# Apple Tart

## (Tarta de Manzana)

3 medium apples
½ c. plain yogurt
⅓ cup sugar
2 eggs

⅓ cup flour
Pinch salt
¼ tsp. baking powder
¼ cup apricot marmalade

Grease and flour a pie plate. Peel and chop one apple in small pieces. Peel and thinly slice the other two apples. Set aside.

Mix the yogurt with the sugar, until blended. Add eggs and mix in well. Mix together the flour, salt and baking powder, then blend well into yogurt mixture. Stir in the chopped apple. Pour batter into the pie plate. Decoratively arrange the apple slices over the entire top of batter. Bake at 350º for 35 minutes, or until pie is set. Remove from oven, and spread marmalade over the apple slices. Let cool. Serves 6.

*María Carmen Luque Martínez*


# Camas Church Cookie Pie

## (Tarta de Galletas de la Iglesia de Camas)

1 family-sized box of chocolate
  pudding and pie filling
1 family-sized box of vanilla pudding
  and pie filling
milk for pie filling

2 c. milk
2 T. anisette liqueur or
  ⅛ tsp. anise seeds
1 large box vanilla wafers

Make both pie mixes according to pkg. directions for pies. Let chill. Pour 2 c. milk in a wide-mouthed bowl. Add 2 T. anisette; or if not available, spoon 1/8 tsp. slightly crushed anise seeds in a tea ball and place in milk. If using the seeds, warm the milk to just scalding, then cool and let steep 10 minutes with seeds. Divide vanilla wafers into 4 parts. Dip one part quickly in milk and lay in the bottom of a greased springform pan. Line the entire pan with wafers. Pour over half the chilled vanilla pie filling. Line again with wafers. Pour over half the chocolate pie filling. Line with wafers, pour over the rest of the vanilla and line with wafers once more. Cover and chill 3-4 hours. When well-set, remove sides of pan and place large cake plate upside-down over the pie.

Flip the pie over onto the plate and carefully remove the bottom of the pan, leaving wafers intact. Spread the last half of chocolate pie filling over the top and sides of the pie. Chill once more until all well-set. Serves 10-12.

*Salud Borrego Méndez*

# Little Pastry Rings

## (Rosquillas)

1½ cup salad oil, separated
2 eggs, whipped till light
½ cup milk
2 tsp. baking powder
⅔ cup sugar

½ tsp. salt
4-5 cups plain flour
1 whole lemon peel, cut in 5-6 pieces
1 tsp. anise seed (optional)
Sugar for dredging rings

Whip eggs in a large bowl. Add milk and blend gently. Mix together dry ingredients, and add to egg and milk, blending thoroughly, but gently. Add enough flour to dough so that when stirred, it begins to leave the edges of the bowl. Turn onto a flour coated surface and knead until fairly smooth (4-5 minutes), adding flour to dough as needed to prevent excessive stickiness. Let dough rest for one hour in original bowl. Remove dough and place on floured surface again, and roll into one long rope 2 inches in diameter. Slice off about twenty ½ inch slices. Take each and roll into a smaller "snake," then press the two ends together to form a ring. Set rings aside on plates. In a heavy, medium frying pan, heat 1 cup oil over medium high heat. Fry the lemon peel (and anise seed if used) until golden brown, strain out and discard. Fill a bowl with 1 cup sugar for dredging rings after frying. Fry 2-3 rings at one time until golden brown, turning after a minute to brown the other side. Test one ring to make sure that the centers are cooking through. Decrease heat and increase frying time if rings are still doughy inside. After frying, remove rings from oil, let rest briefly on paper towel, and then dredge each in bowl of sugar.

*María del Carmen Navarro García*

# Fried Cookies

## (Galletas Fritas)

2 cups of egg custard, OR 1 small package French Vanilla pudding and pie filling mix may be used as a substitution
40 María cookies (flat vanilla cookies, found in the International food section)

Milk required for pie filling
1 cup milk, for dipping cookies
1 tsp. vanilla
2 egg whites
Frying oil
Sugar

# Fried Cookies

*(Galletas Fritas)*

Prepare cookie filling, either custard or vanilla pie filling mix. If using pie filling, prepare according to package directions for pies. Set filling aside. Beat egg whites till frothy. In a medium frying pan, heat oil to medium hot, but not smoking. Warm (but not scald) 1 cup milk, add vanilla. Quickly dip a cookie in milk, spread one tablespoon of pie filling on cookie, and top with a second moistened cookie. Roll the edges of the filled cookie in egg whites. Fry briefly in hot oil until golden on both sides. Remove and roll entire fried cookie in sugar and let cool on plate.

*From several friends*

# Cheese Tart

*(Tarta de Queso)*

| | |
|---|---|
| 1 ½ c. sugar, divided | 16 oz. ricotta cheese |
| 6 oz. graham cracker crumbs | ½ c. plain yogurt |
| ¾ stick butter, melted | ¼ c. sweetened condensed milk |
| ½ c. water, warmed | 1 small pkg. strawberry-flavored |
| 1 pkt. (1 T. or ¼ oz.) |    gelatin |
|    unflavored gelatin | |

Mix ½ c. sugar in a bowl with graham cracker crumbs and melted butter. Press crumb mixture evenly into a pie shell around bottom and sides. In a bowl, mix unflavored gelatin with water according to package directions to soften (no more than ½ c. warm water). To this, add the cheese, the 1 remaining cup sugar, yogurt, and milk. Blend well. Chill. Make strawberry gelatin according to package directions. Cool. Before gelatin is set, pour needed amount for topping on the top of the chilled tart. Be careful not to stir the tart. Smooth and let chill in refrigerator until all well set. Serves 8.

*Loli Angulo Rodríguez*

# Fruit Spears with Yogurt

*(Brocheta de Frutas con Yogur)*

2 peaches, peeled and diced
1 c. kiwi, peeled and diced
1 c. raspberries, strawberries
   and/or cherries

2 T. fat free yogurt
1 T. sugar
juice of one orange

     Peel and dice peaches and kiwi. Alternating fruits, spear chunks of fruit on skewers and spread on a tray. Whisk together yogurt, sugar and juice in a bowl. Pour over top of fruit spears just before serving. Serves 4-6.

*Adela Pineda Camino*


# Baked Apples

*(Manzanas al Horno)*

4 apples
4 T. fruit cocktail

1 c. apple juice

     Core apples and fill with 1 T. each of fruit cocktail. Place separated in baking dish and pour apple juice over fruit. Bake at 350° for 30 minutes, basting every 10 minutes with juice. Serves 8-10.

*Adela Pineda Camino*

# SAUCES, GRAVIES & SANDWICHES

# Spicy Salsa for Meat

*(Mojo Picón)*

1 c. olive oil
1 T. red wine vinegar
¼ c. oregano
1 T. cumin
½ tsp. black pepper
1 T. paprika

1 tsp. sugar
1 small red hot chili pepper
2 tsp. coarse salt
2 T. bread crumbs
¼ c. tomato sauce
3-4 cloves garlic

Put all ingredients in a blender and purée. Makes 2 cups.

*Paula Pérez Benítez*


# Chicken Marinade

*(Salsa para Pollo)*

juice of 2 oranges
juice of 1 lemon

water, equal to the quantity of juices
¼ tsp. salt

Stir together. Pour marinade over uncooked chicken pieces and bake or cook in it. Baste chicken every 15 minutes if baking.

*Dora Ruíz Ortíz*


# Meat Gravy

*(Salsa para Carne)*

1 bulb garlic, peeled and minced
2 large onions, chopped
2-3 cloves
1 bay leaf

½ c. olive oil
1 c. white wine
1 tsp. salt

Sauté garlic and onion together with bay leaf and cloves in olive oil, until soft. Add white wine, remove bay leaf and cloves. Cook 5 minutes more. Pour into blender and purée.

*Dora Ruíz Ortíz*

# All-Purpose Vinaigrette

*(Salsa Vinagreta)*

2 eggs, hard-boiled and chopped
1 onion, minced
5-6 stalks parsley, snipped
1 c. olive oil

1 c. white wine vinegar
1 c. water
1 T. salt

Mix all well and use. Makes 1 qt.

*Salud Borrego Méndez*

# Ali-Oli Dressing

(Mayonesa Ali-Oli)

1 lg. egg
½ clove garlic, minced
½ tsp. lemon juice

1 stalk parsley, minced
½ tsp. salt
⅓ – ½ c. olive oil

In small mixing bowl, mix first five ingredients. Very slowly, pour a thin stream of the olive oil into the mixing bowl while whipping on high speed. Add the oil only as long as the egg mixture is whipping up fluffy. If mixture becomes too thin, temporarily stop adding oil until mixture is once again fluffy. Do not add more than ½ cup olive oil per egg. Mixture is ready when it has the consistency of a pudding. After refrigeration, dressing will be somewhat stiffer. Makes 1 cup.

*Rosa Garrido Serrano*

# Plum Jam

*(Mermelada de Ciruela)*

2 lbs. plums (or peaches or strawberries)      1 lb. brown sugar

Peel and pit fruit. Put in heavy pot to cook over low heat. When it becomes very soft (almost a purée), add brown sugar. Let come to boil and cook 10 minutes more, stirring with a wooden spoon. Let cool. Spoon into canning jars and seal in a water bath 20 minutes for pint jars, 25 if using quart-sized. Makes about 2 pints jam.

*Joaquina Berengena García*

# Tomato Sauce

*(Tomate Frito)*

1 green or red bell pepper, seeded
1 onion
3 lbs. tomatoes, peeled

⅓ c. olive oil
1 T. sugar
1 tsp. salt

Purée pepper and onion in blender. Pour into hot oil in frying pan and let cook over medium-low for 10 minutes. Purée tomatoes. Add to pepper and onion. Let cook 10 minutes covered, stirring from time to time. Add sugar and salt and blend well. Makes 2-2 ½ cups.

*Joaquina Berengena García*


# Dippin' for Bread

*(Pringá)*

1 Chickpea Stew or other meat stew recipe with chickpeas

4-6 loaves of short baguettes

While simmering the stew, set apart a little meat and chickpeas for each person on a small plate. Mash the meat and peas with a fork and mix together. Tear off bread and use it to eat the meat and peas. Serves 4-6.

*Paula Pérez Benítez*


# Workingman's Breakfast Crumbs

*(Migas)*

1-2 c. olive oil for frying
2 bulbs garlic

1 long baguette
2-4 oz. chorizo sausage or
   bacon, diced

# Workingman's Breakfast Crumbs

*(Migas)*

Peel garlic cloves but leave whole. Crumble the baguette, using only the inner white part. In a large frying pan, heat 1 c. oil and sauté garlic until golden. Add the bread crumbs to the pan and fry. As bread fries, continue to break it apart even more with a fork or spatula. In with the frying bread, fry the chorizo or bacon, mixing as well. Add oil as needed to keep bread from sticking. When bread is crispy, the migas are done. Serves 4-6.

*María José Guerrero Abril*

# Seafood Spread

*(Paté)*

3-4 oz. canned mussels, drained
3-4 oz. canned tuna, drained

3 foil-wrapped triangles of soft white cheese, or
4 oz. spreadable soft white cheese

Blend seafood and cheese together in a mixer or blender. Chill. Makes 1 cup.

*Lola Mesa Rodríguez*

# Jumbo Pork Sandwich

*(Montadito)*

1 baguette, 8-10 inches long
1 large pork loin fillet
1 Anaheim green pepper, cleaned

2 T. olive oil
2-3 T. mayonnaise

Fry pork loin and green pepper in olive oil at same time. Let pepper soften and become flat. Halve bread lengthwise and spread mayonnaise on bread. When pork and pepper are both done and tender, place on one side of bread, top with other half. Heat 5 minutes in an oven to warm bread. Serves 1.

*Lola Mesa Rodríguez*

# Smoked Fish Sandwich

---

*(Montadito)*

1 baguette, 8-10 inches long
1 fillet of smoked fish, such as
   salmon
1 Anaheim green pepper,
   cleaned

2 T. olive oil
2-3 slices fresh cheese, such as
   ricotta or cream cheese

Halve the bread lengthwise. Sauté green pepper in hot oil. Set fish on bottom half of bread, then the green pepper, then finally the fresh cheese to cover. Top with other bread half. Heat in oven for 5 minutes to warm sandwich. Serves 1.

*Lola Mesa Rodríguez*

# Shrimp Sandwich

---

*(Bocadillo de Gambas)*

1 short baguette, halved lengthwise
2 T. mayonnaise

8 large shrimp, minced

Mix mayonnaise and shrimp and spread between bread halves. Serves 1.

*Encarni Domínguez Ledesma*

# Salmon Cheese Sandwich

---

*(Bocadillo de Salmón)*

1 baguette, 8-10 inches long
3-4 slices fresh cheese, such as
   ricotta

1 long slice smoked salmon
   or marinated salmon

Halve bread lengthwise. Lay cheese and salmon on one half and cover with the other half. Serves 1.

*Encarni Domínguez Ledesma*

# Appendix

## Tapas Sevillana Style

If you would like to try Spanish snacks or appetizers, called tapas, prepare one of the following cookbook recipes, only reducing the portion size. Serve with olives and crunchy crackers on a small salad plate.

Pork Loins a la Whiskey
Pork Loin in Sherry Sauce
Meat Balls with Vegetables and Gravy
Spanish Omelet
Tortilla with Garlic
Joaquina's Hake
Hake Sauté
Basque Hake
Marinated Dogfish (Shark)
Fried Squid
Potatoes and Squid
Roasted Sardines
Gómez Family Gazpacho
Creamy Summer Soup
Roasted Sweet Peppers
Chopped Salad
Marinated Salad
Marinated Roe Salad
Seafood Splash
Russian Salad
House Bread
Bread with Codfish Spread
Feisty Potatoes
Eggplant Sandwiches
Molasses Sweetened Fried Eggplant
Little Garden Birds
Croquettes

# Notes on Foods and Terms Used

**Olive Oil** – Use an extra-virgin oil rich in deep yellow-green color, promoted for its fruity, intense flavor.

**Cured Ham** – Similar to Italian prosciutto ham, a drained fresh pork leg passes a salt-curing process of some 50-90 days. The process continues with washing, drying, and air curing under strict temperature and humidity conditions. A food high in unsaturated fatty acids, proteins and minerals, ham is sliced in wafer-thin sheets and may be eaten as is, or cooked. An even more flavorful ham comes from acorn-fed mountain pigs and may be cured up to 3 years. An internet search for *Jamón Serrano* or *Ibérico* will reveal information and pictures of these delicious meats which come from the world's number one cured ham producing country.

**Chorizo** – Similar to pepperoni, this hard sausage is commonly eaten as an appetizer, in sandwiches, or included in recipes. It is mainly seasoned with salt, paprika and garlic.

**Coarse Salt** – A large-grain salt that is slightly larger than kosher salt. Spaniards call it fat salt.

**Vinegar** – Use the vinegar suggested, either from red or white wine or sherry vinegar. Plain white vinegar will not give the same flavor.

**Cheese** – Sheep and goat cheeses rank as the most popular. The foil-wrapped soft, triangular cheeses mentioned in the book, such as Laughing Cow® brand cheese, are made from cow's milk and come in a small round cardboard box, with eight in each.

**Squid** – Use a smaller variety to cut in rings and fry, and a larger kind to stew with potatoes.

**Anaheim Green Pepper** (Also called Italian pepper) - This is a long, slightly crooked, sweet variety (not hot) used often in sautés.

**Fish** – Hake is a mild white fish in the cod family. Dogfish is a small, tender shark. Other shark may be substituted in its place.

**Tapas** – A popular mid-evening snack or appetizer eaten in small diners/bars on the street. Create your own tapa by making one of the many appetizers, salads, or main dishes found in this book, only reducing the quantity, and serve alongside chips, French fries, or bread sticks on a small plate.

**Sofrito** – The name for the vegetable sauté often made in conjunction with main dishes, containing onions, garlic, peppers, carrots, etc. Basic to good Andalucían cooking, it is often used as a meat sauce, instead of flour-based gravy.

**Tortilla** – This tasty omelet is usually made of eggs and potatoes, but often contains other ingredients as well. It is a basic Andalucían soul food. Use only olive oil to cook it.

# Index